T H E

1 2 3 4 5

T O P

6 7 8 9 10

T E N

3

P   O   R   S

SIX CYLINDE

S C H E

SUPERCARS

First published in 1992 by
Top Ten Publishing Corporation,
42 Digital Drive, Suite 5,
Novato, California 94949, USA

Printed and bound in
Hong Kong.

The information contained in
this publication is correct to the
best of our knowledge. Both
author and publisher, however,
disclaim any liability incurred as
a result of its use. The publisher
acknowledges that certain words
and model designations are
the property of the trademark
holder. This book is not an
official publication.

ISBN 1-879301-02-4

Probing for the Ultimate, a Timeless Pursuit...

Every object has its rank: The best, the worst, the first, the last, the cheapest, the most expensive, the ugliest, the most beautiful—and all the grades in between. Probing for the best, even the best of the worst, is a timeless pursuit.

The automotive enthusiast is certainly no stranger to the idea. From serious show judging to the car magazine's annual issues featuring the best new cars, the ultimate is always sought.

In book publishing, no such attempt had been made—not until the introduction of our Top Ten Series and its first title on Ferrari. Corvette was the subject of our second effort. Now, in our third title, we turn the focus on six-cylinder Porsches.

But first a few thoughts on the criteria used in the Top Ten selection process:

Style and engineering. The forms that combine to create the look of a car are important. The engineering components that make it perform are important. One could argue that the latter would seem more vital. After all, what good is a contrivance of practical intent if it does not live up to its purpose?

Viewing an automobile from the standpoint of its historic stature, however, requires that both criteria be considered and judged equally important. The automobile is one of the premier showcases of industrial art.

History. First, a model, as a group, is ranked according to the criteria outlined above.

Then comes the search for the factor that sends a particular car to the front row. It can be racing history. Or it can be the first of the breed. Or the last. Or it can be an owner whose story adds nostalgia.

Condition. The ultimate is for an old car to still be in a state of like-new condition. But this is, depending on the era, virtually impossible to find. At best, on rare occasions, this deterioration process can create the super-ultimate: a car that blends new and old—call it patina.

Two levels down from the super-ultimate—one notch down from the ultimate—comes the perfectly restored machine, the one considering history and its quirks, not only the matter of renewal and cold facts.

In the end, there is no such thing as a perfect list. One produced by objective experts runs the chance of being just as controversial as one generated by a subjective individual.

So, here is our list of the Top Ten Porsches. Regardless of your personal preferences, we hope you will enjoy the selection.

CONTENTS

The Top Ten

7

PAGE 86

7

1989 930

A Manhattan man lucked out and got the last Slantnose and the last Turbo wrapped up in one half-million dollar package. It took a machine gun toting guard to keep it safe during the air transportation.

PAGE 114

10

1991 Turbo

Turbo power was the Porsche success story of the seventies. The Turbo for the nineties takes the theme one step further and is the best Turbo yet—a true Top Ten finalist. We pick one of the first one hundred built.

PAGE 94

8

1989 Speedster

It became a collectors item from day one. Many were put away, having never set wheels on the road. Our Top Ten car would have none of that—it had its day in the sun on the French Riviera.

PAGE 70

6

1986 959

More than showcasing Porsche know-how, the 959 prepared the 911 for the nineties. Seven pre-production copies were built. One of them belongs to 959 creator Helmuth Bott. We went to Germany to drive his car.

PAGE 104

9

1990 Carrera 4 RS

The Carrera 4 Lightweight—or RS, as it has also been called—is both the most rare and the most formidable of the new 911s. Less than a dozen have been built. We found Number One, owned by Frank Gallogly.

The Six Cylinder Supercars

The Porsche, that round little creation that made such a tentative entrance on the sports car scene in 1948—appearing while war ravaged Europe was still struggling to get back on its feet—sprang from a visionary concept that exemplified both genius and originality.

Professor Ferdinand Porsche, whose radical solutions had made him one of the brightest stars on the prewar automotive sky, left his son, Ferry, with a legacy of a lifetime. The young man assumed this legacy and applied it to his own dream of manufacturing a sports car carrying the family name.

The novelty of the engineering concept, teamed with the state-of-the-art styling—inspired by the most advanced aerodynamic principles—produced a sports car of outstanding distinction.

The emergence of postwar prosperity caused a surge in the fortunes of the fledgling Porsche organization. This and successes on the race track combined to turn Porsche into one of the most formidable new names on the automotive horizon.

But doing it once would not be enough. Postwar history abounds with illustrations of sports car builders who lost their touch. The concepts that once set these products apart from the competition were ultimately compromised—to the point where enthusiast loyalty disappeared and markets vanished.

This could very well have happened to Porsche. In the end, however, it was the stubborn persistence of the founding father that foiled such a scenario.

Crossroads and watersheds were numerous. Forceful voices from time to time caused a momentary deviation from the course. But Ferry inevitably returned to the pure concept that had guided the company since its earliest days.

In retrospect, no decision was more important than the one that cleared the way for the 356 successor: the 911. A number of directions were explored, one of which would with certainty have led to a disintegration of the purist pattern. When the dust settled, however, the sacred Porsche heritage and its unique concept remained.

With the succession question out of the way, there were still a series of pitfalls along the road. The Porsche purity of thought had to be asserted continuously. Without it, the characteristics that were bred into the 356 and procreated in the 911, could never have been passed on to the next generation. Past the age when most men have sought

More than two decades separate the two plant interiors pictured on these pages. Opposite page, the 911 assembly line in the late sixties. The premises were the same as used to build the 356, and were obtained by Porsche in the 1963 Reutter purchase. To the left, the Roesslebau facility. In this illustration, photographed in 1989, a 911 Speedster receives the finishing touches. Below, the low windshield of the Speedster gives new life to the aging silhouette.

It is this complete absence of artificial enhancement that gives this car the edge over all others we researched...

Developed in the early sixties, the six-cylinder Porsche masterpiece is still going strong. Pictured below, it is seen in its latest configuration as fitted in the new generation 911 Carrera 4. To the right, one of the first renderings detailing the 959 concept. This portion is part of a larger set of drawings, measuring approximately two by eight feet. We found it attached to one of the walls in Bott's garage, where it was photographed for this publication.

solace in retirement, Ferry—who at the time of this writing was exactly one week away from his eighty-third birthday—continues to set the course of the company, now with Wolfgang, youngest of the sons, by his side.

It is this incredible consistency of purpose, combined with the novelty of the original idea, that sets the Porsche apart from the rest, that keeps the faithful in the fold and new converts joining at a steady rate.

More than four decades of creative activity in Zuffenhausen and Weissach, has placed a grand collection of machines on road and track, an output that has already filled volumes with written words and photographed images, and will undoubtedly continue to do so.

With this latest book in the Top Ten series, we take a closer look at the absolute cream of the 911 crop. The period covers almost three decades and saw the parallel emergence of race and road machines—actually, road machines that were often thinly disguised racers.

First in our Top Ten lineup comes a pristine example of the model that started it all, the 911. This model is commonly thought of as having debuted in 1965. There was, however, a short run of just over 200 units

completed late in 1964. We managed to locate a handful of these early 911s, and chose the best of the survivors, a car so original that only a paint job stands between the way it looks now and the way it appeared when it rolled off the line twenty-seven years ago.

Our choice for the second spot in the Top Ten lineup, is a car that represents Porsche's venture into the "homologation special" category. This turned a street 911 into a pure racing machine. Referred to as the 911 R, this model, of which only twenty were built, cleared the way for Porsche's first authentic homologation special: the RS Carrera. This model becomes the third in our Top Ten lineup. The particular example chosen came to our attention after a careful survey of all the cars listed in the International RS Register. With its unspectacular past, which was spent in the quiet care of true enthusiasts, this example could easily have been overlooked. It is this complete absence of artificial enhancement, however, that gives the car an edge over all others we researched.

For the fourth selection in our Top Ten lineup, we chose a car that, although it certainly represents the best of the breed, stands out not only because

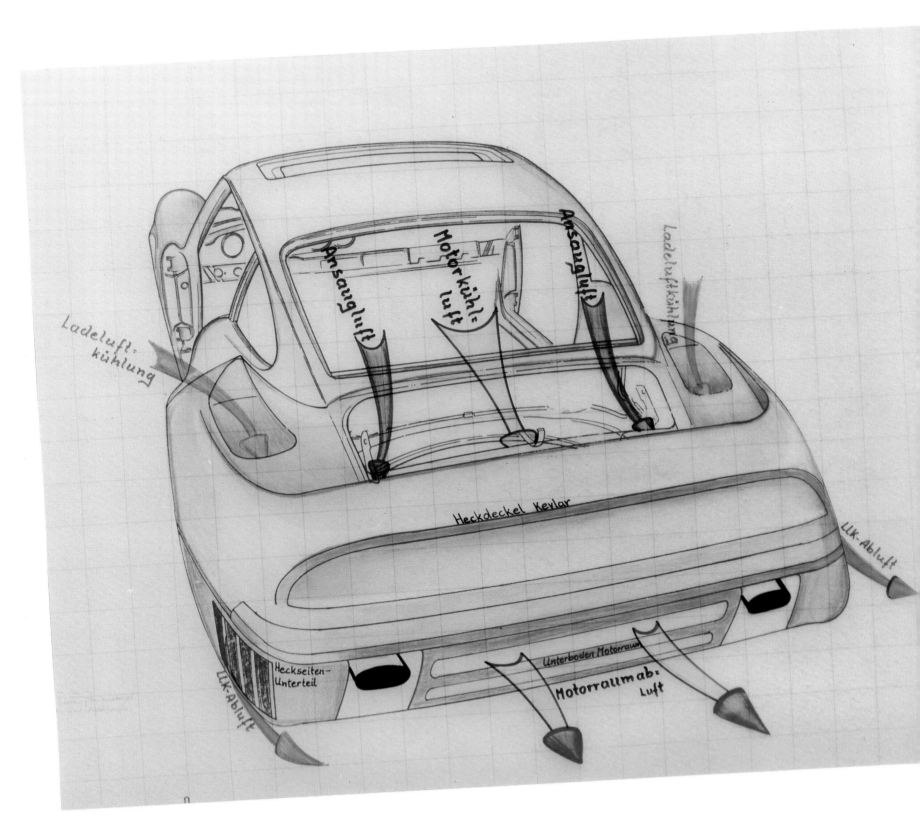

Ladeluft-
kühlung

Ansaugluft

Motorkühl-
luft

Ansaugluft

Ladeluftkühlung

Heckdeckel Kevlar

LLK-Abluft

Heckseiten-
Unterteil

Unterboden Motorraum

Motorraum ab-
luft

LLK-Abluft

INTRODUCTION

The encounter with man and machine stands out as one of the high points among many memorable experiences...

Images such as the black and white photograph below, fill the annals of European rally competition in the late sixties and early seventies. Porsche's ferocious 911s were everywhere. Here Waldegaard and Helmer leave a trail of dust as they storm towards victory in the 1970 Alpine Rally. Opposite, the latest 911 from Porsche's racing department, the Carrera 4 RS. The frontal aspect has changed surprisingly little in the course of two decades.

of the fact that it is the most powerful of Porsche's non-turbo road cars, but also because it has a glamourous past, having once belonged to James Hunt, the Formula One champion.

Fifth in the lineup comes the first known U.S. specification Turbo. Having once served duty in type approval tests, it now resides in Beverly Hills.

Our sixth choice represents a summit on the Porsche road of engineering achievements: the fabulous 959. The featured car belongs to the man who supervised its creation, veteran development wizard Helmuth Bott. My encounter with man and machine stands out as a high point among many memorable experiences.

To occupy the seventh spot, we chose a car that exemplifies the end of an era. Being both the last 930 Turbo and the last Slantnose, the factory spared no effort in making this machine a monument to craftsmanship. As is the case with many of the cars featured, our Top Ten photo session brings this 930 to the public for the first time.

As number eight in our lineup we chose a car that represents the deliberate return to the past, a 911 Speedster, which captures the feeling of its original 356 namesake, although not quite its

looks. Our Top Ten pick staked its claim to fame when, fresh off the line, it was selected by Porsche to star in a photo shoot on the French Riviera.

The ninth Top Ten feature is so rare that it has not been given an official designation. Called both Carrera 4 Lightweight and Carrera 4 RS, this machine has so far been reproduced only a dozen times. We chose the first of the few.

Last in the lineup comes one of the premier examples of the new Turbo, a machine that tells us all is well with the 911—in fact, better than ever.

In previous Top Ten books, I set a precedence by picking my individual favorite, the Top One, if you will. Risking the wrath of some, I will do so again.

It was indeed difficult to pass over the 959, that paragon of engineering prowess. However, nostalgia got the best of me, and I fell for the '73 Carrera RS. Powerful, beautiful, purposeful, this machine represents purity and simplicity at its best.

It is my hope that the perusal of these pages will produce both inspiration and pleasure.

Henry Rasmussen,
San Francisco, September, 1991.

1964 911

Progenitor of Porsche's Six Cylinder Supercars

The Porsche story, as it relates to the manufacture of the Porsche sports car, began in 1947. On June 11 that year, Ferry Porsche and Karl Rabe put pencils to paper in an effort to draw up plans for a roadster relying heavily on Volkswagen components. The design, altered and improved, would take the sports car world by storm. A legend was born: the 356.

Although less than five dozen cars had been built by the end of 1950, and, as Ferry Porsche later reflected, "profits went from zero back to zero" during this formative period, such was the staying power of the 356 that by March 1954, the work force at Porsche's Zuffenhausen factory could celebrate the completion of its 5,000th unit.

In 1959, at a time when the 356 entered its eleventh year and had reached 25,000 in total production, Ferry Porsche came to the conclusion that work on a new model—an effort carried on intermittently since 1955—should be intensified. With this in mind, he gave his oldest son Butzi the go-ahead to draft a conclusive design, one that would become the first volume-produced Porsche road car derived totally in-house.

The path that led to the new model, however, was not without detours. One of the most critical hurdles concerned its basic concept. That the new Porsche should be roomier than the old was evident from the beginning. But there were strong voices within the company arguing that the market for a two-seater would soon be saturated. As a result, when the first prototype set out on its maiden voyage in December 1961, it rolled on a 94.5-inch wheelbase—which was a foot longer than the car whose place it was supposed to take—and featured seating for four adults. Consequently, this design could not be considered a logical replacement for the 356.

Faced with a watershed decision, Ferry Porsche elected to cancel the four-seater project and shift direction toward a two-seater. In so doing, he reconfirmed his faith in the formula that had guided the firm from its earliest days: Porsche was in business to build pure sports cars, nothing less. The path was cleared for the birth of another legend: the 911.

Ferdinand Alexander Porsche was born on December 11, 1935. Like his father, who had been christened Ferdinand Anton Ernst, but was called Ferry, the oldest son received a nickname as well: Butzi.

The 911 was a well-kept secret until a German weekly ran the photo to the left, showing a carefully disguised prototype testing at Nurburgring during the summer of 1963. The real thing made its public debut at the Frankfurt show, opening on September 12. The new Porsche was a crowd pleaser right from the start, as can be seen in the picture on the *opposite* page. Below, our Top Ten feature car is one of the first production 911s.

Overshadowing all other accomplishments of this third-generation Porsche genius, however, is his evergreen 911...

The slim new silhouette of the 911, compared to the rotund features of the aging 356, was not only the result of actual numbers--the 911 added five inches to the wheelbase and nine inches to the length--but also due to the tighter curves prescribed by its designer, Butzi Porsche. To the right, the vital statistics of the 911 as they appear on a 1964 press release rendering. In 1969, the wheelbase was increased by two inches.

Butzi was a headstrong young man, and when the time came to choose a profession, he opted to develop his artistic talent rather than, as was the family tradition, his engineering aptitude.

When Butzi joined Porsche in May of 1957, he was the first family member to follow his father into the business. He held posts in various departments before taking on his assignment of choice in the styling studio. Here he produced the exterior shape of Porsche's forays into open-wheel racing. Later, with the 904, Butzi's talent was displayed in a formidable way.

Overshadowing all other accomplishments of this third-generation Porsche genius, however, is his evergreen 911. The fact that the basic shape is still with us after nearly three decades of changing fashion, speaks for itself. Furthermore, with Porsche's recent investment in the 911 model, the end of this perennial favorite seems nowhere in sight.

O nce Ferry Porsche had set a revised course for the new model, work progressed rapidly. During the summer of 1963, a thoroughly disguised prototype was spotted while being tested at the Nurburgring. Shrouded in an array of fiberglass fakery—such as a set of outrageous fins at the rear and a conspicuous grille up front—the prototype nevertheless revealed the new Porsche to be both longer and sleeker than the model it was to replace. Spy photos of the green monster, published in the German press, whetted the appetite of eager enthusiasts.

T he real thing—Type 901, as it was first referred to—made its official debut at the Frankfurt show in September, 1963.

Britain's venerable *The Motor* hailed it as "perhaps the most notable car at the show", ending its story by predicting that production would not begin "for some time."

This vagueness reflected statements issued by the factory, whose ambivalence in turn stemmed from problems connected with setting up body manufacture. The bottleneck was caused by Karosseriewerk Reutter which, although it had supplied bodies for the 356 almost since the beginning, now balked at the investment required to re-tool for a new model. The problem was resolved when Porsche bought Reutter in 1963.

A small number of prototypes were completed in November that year, but it was not until

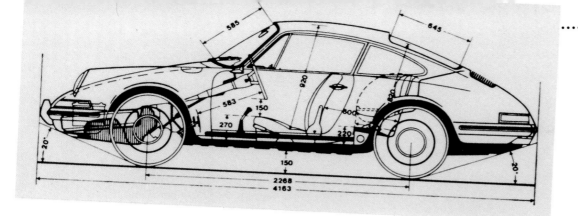

The 695, pictured to the left, rolled on a 94.5-inch wheelbase, featured four seats, and was the forerunner of Butzi's 911. It was not placed in production. Above, left and right, our TopTen choice illustrates the three-quarter front and rear views of Butzi's masterpiece. To the right, a unique photo shows one of the pre-production 911s in the 1964 Tour de France, where it did messenger duty. To the far right, the Linge/Falk equipage gets a new set of tires during the 1965 Monte Carlo rally.

Cummings at first had no clue as to the uniqueness of the car he had purchased...

Butzi Porsche, Ferry Porsche's son, chose the artistic venue instead of the engineering. That his talent was true, and not a pretentious dream, is amply evidenced by his work. The picture below shows Butzi in the styling studio, surrounded by various works in progress. To the right, he poses with his two masterpieces of the early sixties, the 904 and the 911. The color closeup focuses on one of the most pleasing aspects of his 911.

September the following year that series production could be started. To begin with, the assembly line managed only a trickle, and just 232 units were completed before the end of 1964. These early cars were stamped with chassis numbers that started with 300001.

First to drive the brand new Porsche, which by now had received its 911 designation, were members of the motoring press. Their reactions reached American readers with the March and April issues of *Car and Driver,* its enthusiastic reporter hailing it as "the Porsche to end all Porsches", and *Road & Track,* its equally impressed editor ranking it in the "top class among modern GT cars."

One of the first individuals to purchase an example of Porsche's new masterpiece was sports car enthusiast Donald Jennings, an American soldier stationed in Germany. Jennings took delivery of his dream machine on March 23, 1965. The sale was facilitated by E+H Muller, a Porsche dealership located in Worms, the city immortalized by Martin Luther and his reform movement.

Anecdotal evidence seems to suggest that the pre-production prototypes—the exact quantity of which is unknown to this day—were sent back through the assembly line and renumbered. At least one car managed to escape this fate, however, and survives somewhere in Pennsylvania.

This machine, the earliest known 911, would have been the obvious choice for our Top Ten spot, but somewhere along the way the chassis became separated from the original engine; the owner is still in the process of searching for suitable replacement power.

A review of survivors from the 1964 production run, instead focused our attention on chassis number 300134, an exquisitely original example with less than 45,000 miles on the odometer. Since 1975, this survivor has belonged to Bill Cummings, who resides in Soquel, a picturesque California coastal town some sixty miles south of San Francisco.

Cummings at first had no clue to the uniqueness of the car he had purchased. It was only after he instigated the restoration—on an occasion when he took the rear panel Porsche script to a dealer to purchase a new set of fasteners—that he realized what luck had sent his way. The parts man offered him

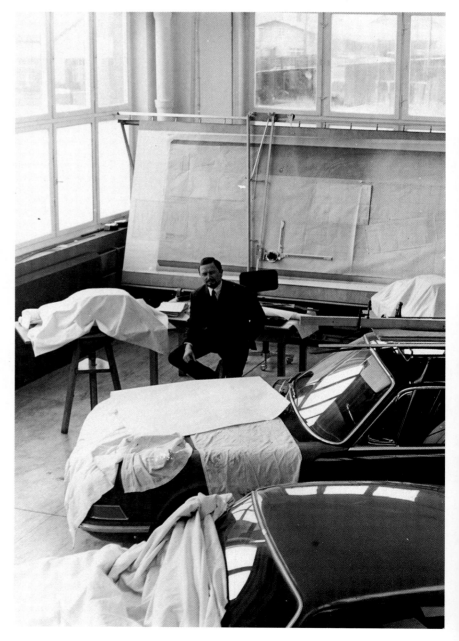

**Further surprises awaited
Cummings as he worked himself
down to the bare metal...**

"seventy-five bucks" for the unique badge, which featured the letters grouped tightly together in one piece and not, as later, spaced far apart and individually attached to the engine lid.

Further surprises awaited Cummings as he worked himself down to the bare metal. For instance, when he separated the front fenders from the rest of the body, he found that the vinyl sealing strips had been cut by hand, a fact evidenced by telltale scissor tracks.

When it came time to apply new paint, Cummings discovered that the original *Rubinrot* was no longer available from the factory. As it happened, a local auto paint shop had saved an old foreign car color paint book which contained the original Porsche paint chips, and was therefore able to produce a perfect match.

This car, then, as pristine and original as one can expect from a twenty-seven-year old machine, is our choice for the Top Ten spot. As seen on these pages, the survivor—never shown anywhere, and never photographed, except in amateur snapshots—stands out as the best among known

examples from the premiere batch of production 911s.

Returning to our story detailing the development of the 356 replacement, we find that in 1962, much of the work still lay ahead.

Amazingly, Butzi was not only able to transform his four-seater into a two-seater, but in the process managed to improve the design. The four-seater featured a front that slanted more aggressively than that of the 356, but was flanked by fenders similar to those found on the predecessor. The rear followed much the same philosophy, building on the past, but appearing slimmer and more streamlined.

Helping to transfer this slimmer line to the two-seater was a new wheelbase, which—measuring 87 inches—was four inches longer than the 356's, although eight inches shorter than the four-seater's.

Butzi retained the front and rear ends of the larger car, but was able to lower the greenhouse. Furthermore, by replacing the four-seater's notchback with a fastback, he managed to move the new design closer to that of the 356, replicating the old machine's characteristically flowing roof,

Porsche sales literature was striking, as exemplified by this 1966 color chart. Nine shades were offered in the U.S.: Slate gray, polo red, golf blue, light ivory, Bahama yellow, Irish green, sand, Aga blue, and black. The seats were red, black, brown or beige, and available in vinyl or optional leather (at extra cost). Vinyl seats were plain, or could be specified with optional basket weave leatherette or hound's tooth fabric inserts.

The 911's dash featured the gauges grouped in a logical and easy-to-read arrangement, with the tachometer occupying center stage, as it should in a true sports car. A touch of class was added through the use of teak wood on dash and steering wheel. To the left, a photograph of one of the earliest production cars. The seats featured hound's tooth inserts, or all vinyl. Above, the dash of our Top Ten survivor. Right, new 911s fill the showrooms in these 1964 scenes.

The final result was a brand new shape, leaner, longer, and more modern, yet one that perpetuated the tradition...

albeit drawing the line more tightly, more disciplined.

The final result was a brand new shape, leaner, longer, and more modern, yet one that perpetuated the Porsche tradition thanks to reassuring touches of familiarity.

Even though the original 911 established a *tour de force* when it came to styling, it was the engineering aspect—as with all Porsches—that formed the heart of the matter.

Consequently, in a parallel to the car's exterior, the engine today remains fundamentally the same as the unit powering the original 911.

Repeating the pattern of development obstacles, the path taken in designing the 911's engine also presented its share of obstacles. It was clear from the start, however, for reasons of improved power and smoothness, the six-cylinder route was the way to go.

The first six-cylinder design emerged under technical director Klaus von Rucker in 1961. The unit owed its basic configuration both to Porsche's eight-cylinder racing engine and to the old four-cylinder Volkswagen motor, retaining push-rod operated valves.

At the end of 1962, von Rucker was replaced by Hans Tomala. The change of leadership prompted a review of the six-cylinder engine; in the end it was deemed both too complicated and too heavy.

The efforts now shifted to a design featuring overhead camshafts. This was a decision of monumental importance to future development, since it incorporated a capacity to cope with the high crankshaft speeds required by the ever-increasing performance demands of both road and racing machines.

The engineering was the work of Ferdinand Piech, a Ferry Porsche nephew who joined the firm in April 1963. His brilliant execution of the overhead camshaft revision was rewarded two years later when he was made head of Porsche's research department.

The revised six-cylinder design featured wet-sump lubrication. But with an eye on the inherent oil surge problems of a boxer engine—where fast cornering results in a rush of oil to one bank of cylinders—this was soon changed to a dry-sump system modeled after Porsche's racing engines. With this last-minute change, the final version of the 911's engine (Porsche design number 901/1), stood ready to be mated to the chassis.

The prototype 901 engine, seen to the right, featured an exhaust system with dual outlets. This was changed for production, with only a single outlet emerging from the left side below the bumper, as in the black-and-white shot on the opposite page. The air cleaner was black, although our *Top Ten* choice, seen below and to the left, features a chromed version. This could have been an aftermarket item. Other U.S. cars have been seen with the same product.

1964 PORSCHE 911

This was the machine popular British motor journalist Denis Jenkinson called "one of the great cars of today by all standards..."

The first test of the 911 came in the 1965 Monte Carlo rally, with Herbert Linge and Peter Falk capturing a second in the GT-class under 2.5 liters. Seen here, the equipage negotiates a hairpin during special trials at La Roquette. Featuring polished ports, higher compression, wilder cams, platinum spark plugs, Weber carbs, lightened flywheel and free-flow exhaust, the engine produced 160 hp, and foreshadowed the S-model.

Ferry Porsche's directives for the 356 replacement demanded increased luggage space, as well as improved handling and ride comfort.

The first objective was accomplished through a new front suspension. Longitudinal torsion bars, bolted to a chassis cross member and a lower wishbone, took care of the springing, while MacPherson struts—lacking conventional coil springs—cared for shock absorption.

For the rear, the transverse torsion bars used on the 356 were kept, but handling and comfort considerations resulted in removal of the old swing-axle in favor of semi-trailing arms.

Amalgamation of chassis, engine and body produced a total weight of 2380 pounds. With the engine putting out 130 hp at 6100 rpm, the new Porsche flagship was capable of a zero-to-sixty time of 8.5 seconds and a top speed of 130 mph.

This was the machine popular British motor journalist Denis Jenkinson called "one of the great cars of today by all standards." It was the machine *Car and Driver* said was "worth the price of all old Porsches put together." And it was the machine that formed the foundation for a development program with few parallels in automotive history.

A postscript to the story is provided by Bill Cummings, owner of our Top Ten choice. With the realization of his car's uniqueness came a desire to know more about its early history. Through the man from whom he bought it, who was the third owner, Cummings was able to ascertain that it had previously belonged to a farmer in Stockton, California, where it had been sitting outdoors in an orchard. It was badly faded, and therefore in need of a new coat of paint.

Further detective attempts uncovered the name of the second owner, and subsequent correspondence produced documents that traced the car to its first owner: the same Donald Jennings mentioned earlier, the American serviceman stationed in Germany, one of the first to buy a 911.

The pristine survivor seen on these pages sets the tone for the continuation of our narrative, and stands out as a progenitor of the remarkable line of sports cars created by some of the world's most talented automotive designers and engineers.

26

1967 911 R

The One that Started the Homologation Specials

The launch of a new model is a traumatic event for any car maker. In addition to the teething problems experienced on the lines of production, there is that all-important bottom line: Will it sell?

In the case of Porsche and its 911, the answer came quickly and unequivocally. The 356 was phased out at the end of 1965, and 1966 became the first full-year test of the new model: 12,820 units were built, which was an annual production record for Porsche.

Adding to the success in the showroom that year was the impressive collection of laurels captured on the race track: outright victory in the Targa Florio added to class wins at Le Mans, Monza, Daytona, and Sebring, to mention only the most prominent. While these victories were won by Porsche's all-out 906 sports racer, the 911 also showed its mettle with wins in major rallys.

Seeing the 911 in action further whetted the appetite of the sports car enthusiasts, who now looked for increased performance in the street machine as well. In what was to become a first installment in the long and incredibly successful 911 development saga, Porsche responded to the enthusiasts' wishes in the

form of the 911S. As a result of improved breathing, output went from 130 hp to 160, zero to 60 from 8.7 seconds to 7.3, and top speed from 130 mph to 137.

But Ferdinand Piech in the research department, and Huschke von Hanstein in the public relations department (where the responsibility for racing management rested in those days), had something much more exciting up their sleeves: the 911R—the R referring to the German word *Rennen*, meaning Racing.

Although the R is generally and correctly classified as a pure racing machine (a species this book planned not to consider), the R's inclusion here is warranted by the fact that it paved the way for future homologation specials. It was a forerunner of that ultimate breed of road Porsches—the kind zooming on the edge between all-out racer and street-legal rocket—which was just the type of machine we were aiming for in our title: Porsche/Six-Cylinder Supercars.

The first four (some sources say three) 911Rs emerged from Porsche's experimental department in the spring of 1967. The concept from which production of these machines was formulated came from the

The Monte Carlo rally became a classic 911 affair, with its 1965 class win repeated in 1967; in the picture on the opposite page, Walter and Lier drift through a sharp turn. In 1968, Elford and Stone took first overall, a feat repeated the next year by Waldegard and Helmer--commemorated in the factory poster. The rally cars led to the R--seen to the left during its 1967 Hockenheim introduction. Below, our Top Ten choice, R number 15.

Lightening measures were drastic, lowering the weight from the road version's 2260 pounds to an incredible 1810 pounds...

question: What would be the effect if we took the existing road car, lightened it as much as possible, then mated it to a power plant fortified along the lines of our most potent six-cylinder competition engine?

The result was most satisfying indeed, as evidenced by the R's immediate racing successes. In July, an R placed third at Mugello, Italy. In August, another R won the *Marathon de la Route* at the Nurburgring. In October, a pair of Rs, piloted by Steinemann/Siffert and Spoerry/Voegele, were taken to Monza, where they proceeded to set five world records in the two-liter class. After ninety hours and 20,000 kilometers of flat-out running, the average speed exceeded 130 mph. These accomplishments justified the decision to produce a batch of twenty additional units to the R specifications.

This group was completed in October, at which time von Hanstein introduced the idea of going on to manufacture 500 units—the number required for homologation as a Grand Touring racing machine.

Von Hanstein believed that, between the cars he could sell to privateer racers and the ones that could be marketed to individual enthusiasts for road use, the project could be most

successful from a financial as well as a public relations viewpoint. In the end, however, von Hanstein was overruled by Lars-Roger Schmidt, the sales manager, who obviously did not see the potential. Ironically, half a dozen years later, von Hanstein was proven right, when the Carrera RS generated sales three times as large.

The actual specifications of the prototype Rs varied somewhat from those governing the production of the October batch of twenty. Due to lack of space, we focus on the latter.

The lightening measures were drastic, lowering the weight from the road version's 2260 pounds to an incredible 1810. In order to accomplish this, Karl Baur—a Stuttgart company contracted by Porsche to make the body alterations—exchanged the standard steel doors, front fenders, front and engine lids, front and rear bumpers, even the taillight assemblies and the dash, for fiberglass replacement components. The rest of the body, for structural rigidity, remained standard.

Further lightening was accomplished through drilling the floorboards, exchanging standard hinges for aluminum ones, replacing the regular door handles with epoxy replicas,

The 911 R rolled on the same Fuchs forged alloy wheels, opposite page, as used on the S-model. Special blinkers and reflectors were used to cut weight. Gaping holes funneled air to a front mounted oil cooler. The rear window, left, was made from Plexiglass. Special bars prevented it from popping out. The Plexiglass rear quarter windows, above, featured a neat row of air vents. The black-and-white shot on the opposite page shows the R that won the 84-hour Marathon de la Route.

A quick glance in the engine compartment produces a rush of pure engineering ecstasy...

The R was powered by the same type of engine (901/20) that made its debut in the 1965 Targa Florio, where it propelled Maglioli's 904. With its double rows of voracious Webers, the engine not only looks capable, but produces 210 horses. Bottom of the page, an R is prepared for a record run at Monza that lasted 96 hours at an average speed of 130 mph. Right, an R lifts a front wheel on the way to victory in the Marathon de la Route.

specifying thinner glass for the windshield, using Plexiglass for side and rear windows, removing the rear seats, floor mats, heater, ashtray, cigar lighter, clock, passenger sunvisor, as well as the standard door panels, and, finally, by replacing the front seats with light-weight racing variants.

The suspension continued the changes made on the S, specifically anti-roll bars up front and at the rear, and externally adjustable Koni shocks. The wheels were also the same as on the S—the attractive Fuchs alloys—but with offset seven-inch rims in the back. The all-around ventilated disc-brakes were carryovers from the S as well. The frame and chassis structures otherwise remained standard.

A glance in the engine compartment produced a rush of pure engineering ecstasy. Fitted in place of the S's power plant (Porsche design number 901/02), was a 901/22 version of the flat six, a machine resembling the 906 racing power plant (901/20), with purposeful high-performance specifications: aluminum or magnesium crankcase, alloy cylinders and cylinder heads, dual ignition, and enlarged valves and ports. The crowning touch was a pair of triple-throat 46 mm Webers, complete with

voracious velocity stacks. Engineered with a compression ratio of 10.3 to one, this masterpiece—emanating directly from Porsche's experimental department—put out 210 hp at a high-pitched 8000 rpm.

The search for a Top Ten finalist was directed by a special set of criteria. First, because of our desire to feature only road cars in this book, we felt it appropriate to purposely stay away from individual Rs with prominent racing histories, and instead treat street use as an important plus. Secondly, since all twenty of the Rs were basically alike, it was desirable to locate an example with some unique characteristic, something that set it apart from the run of the mill—if that expression can be applied to any R.

A review of the serial number listing, which begins with 911899001, and ends with 911899020, focused the spotlight on number 15, a car the records indicated might have been the only example imported directly to the U.S. Most of the Rs were sold in Europe, where a majority still remains today. Eight Rs are thought to presently be in the U.S.

Furthermore, number 15 stood out because of its color;

All the original components were present and intact, and although a bit tired, the old racer was in surprisingly good condition...

the standard was white, while this particular machine was metallic gold. Only one other R is known to have received a special color: number 20, painted blue. This machine is presently in Japan.

Number 15 was found to have been delivered to the Porsche dealer in Alexandria, Virginia on November 29, 1967, earmarked for its owner, Joel Heishman. As the story goes, he chose the special color —which added three weeks to the delivery time—to match his wife's Cadillac. While this may or may not be fact, the fact that Heishman entered number 15 in the 24-Hour race at Daytona—run early in 1968—is indisputable.

Piloted by McDaniel and Sullivan, the car—displaying a large number 3 on its doors and front lid—won its class (for prototypes under two liters), and finished fourteenth overall.

The result might have been more impressive had one of its drivers not flipped the car, which landed on the roof before somersaulting back on its wheels. The acrobatic exhibition was witnessed by Bruce Jennings (known to Porsche enthusiasts as King Carrera), who was driving immediately behind the R at the time. The roof received considerable

damage, but not the pilot, and after a thorough check-up, the number three car was again circling the track, ultimately completing a total of 562 laps.

After the bittersweet interlude at Daytona, number 15 was shipped back to the Virginia dealership, where the damage to the roof received appropriate attention. Apparently the rare survivor was then sold locally, and subsequently changed hands several times, owned by a series of Virginia Porsche collectors.

We next encounter number 15 in West Palm Beach, Florida. It is during this period that its street experience was gained. Running for a number of years on normal Florida registration tags, the car also saw limited action in auto-crosses. In spite of its hard-to-ignore exhaust note, the machine was driven on the street to and from these events.

In the early eighties, number 15 was purchased by Kevin Jeanette, of Gunnar Porsche Racing, located in Jacksonville. Jeanette was impressed by the machine's unadulterated state. All the original components were present and intact, and although a bit tired, the old racer was in surprisingly good condition. Jeanette proceeded with a restoration that was

The R is stripped to the bare minimum. No stone was left unturned in the effort to save weight, as illustrated by the heavily drilled passenger-side floorboard visible in the photograph above. The dashboard is molded from fiberglass and features as its center piece, seen to the left, a 10,000 rpm tachometer, turned for easy viewing in racing fashion. Special Scheel racing seats, pictured to the right, are vented and hold the driver and his passenger in a tight and secure grip.

Its loud, screaming voice comes raspy and raw from deep inside the alloy lungs of the beast...

characterized by a desire to preserve the authenticity of the machine, a philosophy that produced a car that experts on the R insist today looks exactly like it did when it left the Porsche factory.

The next change of ownership saw number 15 delivered into the hands of one of the most consummate Porsche connoisseurs in the world, pioneer sports car enthusiast Miles Collier. As the story goes, the car actually came to Collier via his mother, who bought it for him as a Christmas gift. The year was 1982 or 1983. Collier proceeded to have Bruce Jennings campaign it on the historic racing circuit, where its unique golden physiognomy became a familiar sight.

Today, number 15 belongs to another experienced Porsche collector, Prescott Kelly, of Weston, Connecticut, in whose devoted custody it shares garage space with a number of precious examples of the marque. The odometer shows approximately 13,000 kilometers. Daytona practice accounts for the first 1,000 kilometers, while the actual race would have added 2,000 kilometers more. The rest has accrued over the years—not much for a twenty-four-year old

car. It has indeed lived an exceptionally pampered life.

Kelly occasionally brings his rare survivor to the track, where he says the machine turns heads because of its loud, screaming voice which comes raspy and raw from deep inside the alloy lungs of the beast. Although the acceleration cannot be characterized as neck-snapping, the power available at high rpms is absolutely rivetting, says Kelly. It is important to keep the revs up, he continues, and to keep that shifting arm moving. Moreover, as Kelly has experienced on numerous occasions, the extreme lightness of the car and its wider than standard rubber causes the R to not exhibit as much of the tail-slinging break-away tendency so typical of early 911s. The R is really an easy car to drive, Kelly says, and a most exhilarating one, he adds.

This machine then—original down to the most minute detail, painted by the factory in a unique customer specified shade, the only example known to have been originally exported to the U.S., legally driven on the street for many years, a winner at Daytona, and, finally, exceptionally well restored and preserved—is our choice for the Top Ten spot.

The Porsche engineers went so far in their efforts to lighten the R that they had special plastic door handles made, as seen in the illustration above. The filler cap covers a pipe leading to an oil tank located just ahead of the rear axle. The photograph to the left, closes in on the rear lights. As up front, they are of a plain, lightweight design. The hub cap, the object focused on in the photograph to the right, features a Porsche crest decoratively engraved into the metal.

With pilots McDaniel and Sullivan taking turns behind the wheel, and sponsored by owner Joel Heishman, our *Top Ten* feature managed an impressive showing in the 1968 24-Hour race at Daytona, winning its class. The browning photo to the left, captures it in action. The shot was taken before an unfortunate accident made a mess of the roof. But the damage did not prevent the R from completing all of 562 laps.

1973

911 CARRERA RS

The Purist's Pick Among Production Porsches

The early seventies ushered in a time of change for Porsche, a time to end old ways, a time to begin new adventures.

Organizationally, the period saw top management swept aside. Ferry Porsche had come to the conclusion that family dominance of the decision-making process was limiting the future of the company.

While Porsche's sons and nephews had made tremendous contributions to the company, there had also been inter-family squabbling. The disagreements were, as Ferry Porsche put it, "like sand in a well-oiled machinery." After a June 1971 family council, it was agreed that members of the Porsche clan should no longer hold management positions.

Porsche stepped down from the post of chief executive, naming Ernst Fuhrmann—father of the legendary four-cam engine—as his successor. Butzi Porsche (Ferry's son) moved back to Austria, where he formed his own company, Porsche Design. Ferdinand Piech (Ferry's nephew) went to Audi—in a capacity that gave him responsibility for research and development—leaving his domain at Porsche (development) in the capable hands of Helmuth Bott.

Just as the era of Porsche family dominance in management came to an end, so ended another era—that of the 917 and its rule of the sports racing scene.

Although well worth its astronomical price from a public relations point of view, the 917 program—which brought Porsche the World Championship for Makes three years in a row—was a tremendous financial drain.

It also was clear that Federation Internationale de l'Automobile, which governed racing, would use its power to end the one-make superiority. A rule change, banning five-liter cars, was scheduled to go into effect at the end of 1971. The new formula limited engine capacity to three liters.

While Porsche would reap further glory with its big-engine racing machines in the Can-Am series, it appeared clear to Fuhrmann, who was a firm believer in racing as a means of improving the breed, that a less costly way had to be found.

The answer lay in further development of the 911, a program that gave the sports car world some of its most outstanding examples, and Porsche a model many consider

Since its inception, the 911's tendency to become unstable at high speeds, as well as its sensitivity to side winds, had been well-known facts. In April 1970, the windtunnel at the Stuttgart University was the site of a series of tests which ultimately established the addition of a front air dam and a rear spoiler. The Carrera RS was the first to feature these aerodynamic aids. The poster at the top of the page, proclaims the RS to be "Germany's Fastest Production Sports Car!"

Before the 911 could become truly competitive, three of its major problem areas had to be tackled...

A turn-of-the-century generating station located in London's Winchmore Hills, provides the unusual setting for our Top Ten Carrera RS. The location is in fact a home away from home ("home is on the road" says its owner Fred Hampton) for the completely original and perfectly pristine survivor, as the generating station has been transformed into garage and workshop for Allen Seymour, who stores and cares for the RS.

its ultimate road car: the 911 Carrera RS.

A first step on the road to a racing 911 was a model upping the ante to a more competitive level, a model suitable for homologation—the process by which a car is deemed to conform to racing classification rules. From this level, the ante could be upped once more through further development. Translated into numbers, the first level would produce a car for Group 3, which required 500 units to be built within a twelve-month period; the second level, a car for Group 4, required fifty units.

Before the 911 could become truly competitive, three of its basic problem areas had to be tackled: weight, power, and aerodynamics. With Fuhrmann's blessing, Bott set the ball rolling in May of 1972, placing Norbert Singer in charge of the project.

The first problem area, weight, was tackled by using thinner-gauge steel for doors, roof, front fenders, front lid, and portions of the floor pan.

Thinner glass was specified, replacing the standard front and rear windows, as well as the rear quarter ones. Fiberglass was used for the front and rear bumpers.

Almost all soundproofing was removed, as were rear seats, clock, passenger sunvisor, map reading lamp, and glovebox lid. Standard door panels were exchanged for plain panels, lacking arm rests, and featuring leather pull straps for opening; no-nonsense plastic handles (these units were incidentally the same as used on Fiat's 500) facilitated closing. Normal seats were exchanged for Recaro sport buckets, which had their fiberglass shells covered with black cloth. The rake could be adjusted via thumb screws on either side of the seat.

Additional lightening was accomplished by removing one of the batteries, leaving the other in place on the left side of the spare wheel. These steps saved 210 pounds, and fixed the weight at 1985 pounds.

The next sequence of necessary improvements focused attention on the engine compartment, where a revised power plant produced 210 hp at 6300 rpm, up from 190 at 6500. This was achieved by increasing the bore to 90 mm, up from 84, for a total volume of 2687 cc. The largest bore so far, it could not have been accomplished without the Nikasil cylinder coating process pioneered on the 917. Valve

Only one thing was missing, a catchy name.
For this purpose the legendary
Carrera appellation was dusted off...

sizes, timing, and compression remained unchanged from the S, as did Bosch's mechanical fuel-injection.

Changes to the chassis included a switch from Koni shocks to Bilsteins. Anti-roll bars were stiffened, measuring 18 mm in the front and 19 mm at the back. Fifteen-inch Fuchs alloy wheels were retained, as were six-inch rims up front, while the rear received seven-inch rims. This, and the addition of 7 mm spacers, necessitated flaring the rear fenders.

With these chassis improvements, cornering tests produced a g-force figure of 0.912. This was a record for a production Porsche; no other had broken the 0.9 barrier.

The third sequence of improvements concerned aerodynamics. The Porsche engineers had long been aware of the 911's rear lift problem, which caused high-speed instability and oversteer. Wind tunnel testing revealed that a small "duck tail", mounted immediately below the engine air intake and extending to the approximate height of the rear window sill, reduced lift by about seventy-five percent, to 93 pounds. The tail also affected the drag coefficient, lowering it from 0.41 to 0.40.

For production, the duck tail became part of an integral fiberglass deck lid, which was reinforced by an aluminum frame. Rubber fasteners were used to hold the lid in place.

In this form, the revised 911 stood ready for introduction. Only one thing was missing, a catchy name. For this purpose the legendary Carrera appellation was dusted off and applied via decals to the bottom portion of each side of the body panels as well as to the rear deck lid.

The Carrera RS made its debut at the Paris Salon, which opened on October 5, 1972. Such was the response that even before the end of the event all 500 units had been spoken for. Production had begun in July, but with such convincing evidence of a positive public reaction, another batch of 500 units was added. Before it was all over, in July 1973, a total of 1580 units had been built.

The first ten cars were appropriated by the factory, and are considered to be prototypes. Fifty-seven cars were built to RSR specifications, the racing version, about which more will be said in the next chapter. There were 1319 units built of the Touring variation,

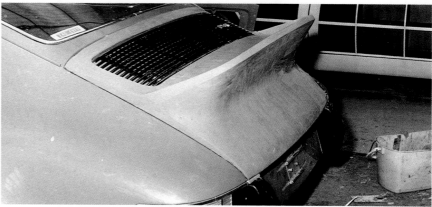

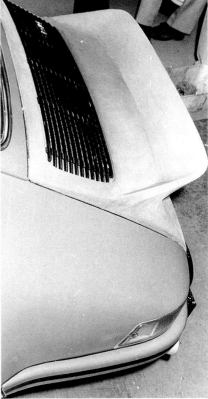

The rare black-and-white photographs on this spread, according to notes scribbled on their backs, were taken in 1972, at a point when the stylists had arrived at the ultimate shape of the ducktail. The color pictures illustrate, opposite page, a portion of the air dam, and on this page, the flared rear wheel arches, necessitated by the seven-inch rims. A deeper dam was tried but while it lowered the overall drag factor it was found to create an undesirable frontal down-thrust.

We were looking for a machine that would be judged solely on the merits of authenticity and condition...

The color shots on this spread offer views of the Carrera cockpit, with its snug Recaro seats, and the engine compartment, with its potent power plant. Nothing has been done to this machine; it is as good as new, and has only 26,000 miles on the clock. The old photos show divergent factory developments on the RS theme. To the right, an early RSR, driven to a ninth at Dijon. Below, an RS for the East African Safari, which it did not finish.

which featured the lightweight body, but with standard bumpers and 911 interior. The remainder, 204 units, were of the Sport type, built according to the basic specifications outlined above. Of these, 103 are listed in the International RS Register. This group, it seemed, would constitute a worthy assemblage of finalists for our Top Ten spot.

The ultimate representative of the RS, we decided, should have no track history. We were looking for a machine that would be judged only on the merits of authenticity and condition, in other words , a car that in its absence of apparent significance—such as being the first or the last or having had a famous owner—expressed ultimate significance.

It was not possible to research, much less inspect, all 103 RSs. After consultations with a number of experts, a handful of cars seemed to fit our criteria. Emerging from this group was one particular machine, chassis 9113601158, belonging to Fred Hampton of London, England.

The car was sold new to a doctor in Milan, Italy, who owned it until 1977, driving it only occasionally. The doctor sold it to a dealer in Italy, who

in turn sold it to a dealer in England. From here it went to an owner who kept it until 1983, during which time it was cared for by Allen Seymour. When the owner wanted to sell, Seymour contacted his friend Hampton, who was quick to close the deal.

No one, not even Hampton, realized the significance of the car at the time. Superficial at first, his fascination soon led to a deeper involvement. It has now reached a point where his findings regarding the RS models, supported by extensive research at the factory, are being put into book form.

This machine, then, number 1158, is our choice for the Top Ten spot. It is unrestored, but authentic and pristine to the point of perfection—a worthy exponent of a Porsche road machine that expresses the honest sports car ideal better than any other of its generation.

With its low weight, accomplished through the elimination of nonessentials, its aerodynamic efficiency, reached through means that broke new ground, and its staggering performance—zero to sixty in 5.5 seconds and a top speed of 153 mph—the RS embodies all the attributes of an automotive legend.

Carrera

1974

911 CARRERA RS

Rarest and Raciest of the Road Porsches

If FIA, the federation ruling international racing, indeed thought it possible to regulate Porsche's dominance of the racing scene by changing the rules, it was seriously mistaken. The creative force of the brains at Weissach, Porsche's new engineering center, was too dynamic to be squashed by the whims of bureaucrats.

The seemingly innocent development of the 911 into the Carrera 2.7 RS road car, its homologation, its subsequent evolution into the formidable Carrera 3.0 RS—the Top Ten car featured here—and the creation of the 2.8 RSR and 3.0 RSR racers, instead opened the floodgates for another wave of Porsche supremacy.

This period of renewed preeminence was launched in February of 1973, with a sensational win at Daytona. Piloted by Peter Gregg, a name that would become synonymous with Porsche racing glory, the Stuttgart firm's prototype 2.8 RSR was so far ahead near the end that a manufacturer of car wax offered a complimentary application of its product to enhance the car's appearance before it crossed the finish line.

Gregg turned down that offer, but not the IMSA Camel GT winner's trophy presented to him at the close of the 1973

season. Porsche and Gregg went on to capture a second IMSA trophy in 1974.

In Europe, Porsche's 2.8 RSR steam roller shifted into high gear at the Nurburgring early in 1973, where two examples of Porsche's new breed were pitted against each other. John Fitzpatrick and Claude Ballot-Lena battled fiercely for first, with the latter finally capturing the honors. The 2.8 RSR kept rolling right through the season, flattening the opposition, and winning the Grand Touring championship.

The era of the 3.0 RSR was ushered in when Herbert Mueller and Gijs van Lennep drove a prototype, painted in the now immortal Martini colors, to a ninth at Dijon in April of 1973. The same duo won Targa Florio in May, giving Porsche its eleventh victory in the event.

The 3.0 RSR, which placed racing teams like Kremer and Loos on the map and made household names of drivers like Clemens Schinkentanz and Hartwig Bertrams, kept up the pressure throughout the 1974 and 1975 seasons, capturing the GT crown both years.

With Martini helping to underwrite the project, Porsche subsequently developed its 3.0 liter machine further, adding

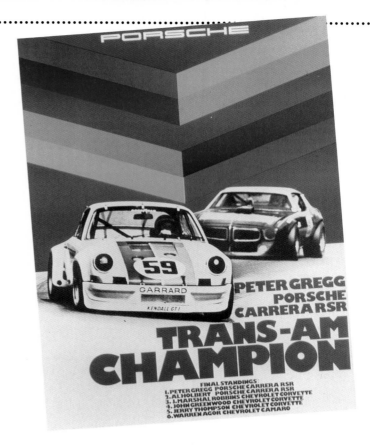

PETER GREGG PORSCHE CARRERA RSR

TRANS-AM CHAMPION

FINAL STANDINGS:
1. PETER GREGG PORSCHE CARRERA RSR
2. AL HOLBERT PORSCHE CARRERA RSR
3. J. MARSHAL ROBBINS CHEVROLET CORVETTE
4. JOHN GREENWOOD CHEVROLET CORVETTE
5. JERRY THOMPSON CHEVROLET CORVETTE
6. WARREN AGOR CHEVROLET CAMARO

A World War II hangar serves as backdrop to our Top Ten 3.0 RS, below. Lord Hesketh, sponsor of his own Formula One team, was original owner. Opposite page, Hesketh with his star driver, James Hunt, who received the RS as part of a settlement when Hesketh withdrew. The factory poster commemorates Peter Gregg's Trans-Am championship. The car he drove to victory at Daytona, left, was a link in the chain that produced the 3.0 RS.

The R stands for Rennen, meaning racing in German. The S stands for Sport, which needs no translation...

Both the 3.0 RS and 3.0 RSR--a factory fresh copy of the latter is readied for photography at Works 1 in the picture at the bottom of the page--were fitted with the latest aerodynamic aids as evolved through racing and windtunnel tests. The front air dam, below, was drawn deeper and fitted with a grille, both measures lowered front lift and allowed a sizeable increase in the rear spoiler, creating the whale tail. Both were indigenous to the RS and the RSR.

ferocious turbo power and far-out aerodynamic aids. These efforts led to the 930 Turbo, and in the end produced the ultimate silhouette racer, the 935.

In order to analyze the development steps that led to the creation of our Top Ten choice—the 3.0 RS—we must take a closer look at the engineering aspects of the 2.8 RSR, which takes us back to October 1972 and the point when Norbert Singer, the man in charge of the project, stood ready to submit his creation to homologation.

Its RSR designation, incidentally, causes confusion even among the cognoscenti. The R stands for *Rennen*, meaning Racing. The S stands for *Sport*, which needs no translation. The second R, however, is said to also stand for Racing, a seeming redundancy.

The 2.8 RSR utilized the same body as the 2.7 RS, which had been lightened through the specification of thinner-gauge steel and glass, the use of fiberglass for certain components, and the removal of comfort features. Up front, the 2.8 RSR incorporated a wider dam, however, which in turn featured a rectangular aperture that funnelled air to a front-mounted oil cooler.

The 2.8 RSR rolled on Fuchs aluminum wheels, 9 inches wide up front and 11 inches at the rear. Disc brakes, lifted from the 917, were vented and drilled.

The suspension had also been revised, and featured relocated spindles up front. In back, the arms were shortened and moved both rearward and outward. The first modification allowed deeper suspension travel, while the second placed the wide rubber more firmly on the road by better matching camber change to body roll.

Changes to the engine included a bore increase from 90 mm to 92 for a total volume of 2808 cc, the installation of Mahle racing pistons, Carrera 6 camshafts and four-bearing cam boxes. Breathing was enhanced through an increase of inlet and exhaust ports from 38 mm to 43, and the fitting of larger valves. Combustion was improved through the specification of twin-plug Marelli ignition. Bosch fuel-injection remained. With a compression of 10.5 to one, the beefed-up power plant produced 308 hp at 8000 rpm. It was the first time the 911 engine passed the 300 hp mark.

This was the machine that provided such a thrilling season opener at Daytona. As we have seen, it went on to fulfill the

One negative aspect of the increased width of the 3.0 RS, as compared to the 2.7 RS, was that performance was only marginally improved...

The massive frontal aspect of the 3.0 RS, opposite page, makes for an impressive sight, and illustrates how far aerodynamic development had brought the 911 without substantially changing the basic shape. Our Top Ten feature car, below, is one of six right-hand drives brought to England. Seen at the bottom of the page, a left-hand drive tested by Road&Track. To the right, a 3.0 RS circling the track at Porsche's Weissach facility.

high hopes of the management, from Ernst Fuhrmann at the top, to Helmuth Bott at development, down to Herr Singer. Altogether, 48 of the 1580 2.7 RSs were turned into 2.8 RSRs.

The further development of the 2.8 RSR grew out of Porsche's need to meet the stronger competition anticipated in 1974. A fortunate paragraph in the rule book allowed a manufacturer to produce an "evolutionary" version of a homologated model. To qualify, just 100 units had to be built. It was through this crack Porsche managed to squeeze the most powerful of its seventies road cars, the 3.0 RS, and one of its most awesome all-out GT racers, the 3.0 RSR.

The 3.0 RS, although its designation seemed to relate it directly to the 2.7 RS, was in reality closer to the 2.8 RSR. The engine had been bored out further, to 95 mm, producing a volume of 2994 cc. Valve and port sizes corresponded to those of the 2.7 RS engine, while the four-bearing cam boxes and shafts, as well as the dry sump oil system, came from the 2.8 RSR. With a 9.8 to one compression, output was 230 hp at 6200 rpm.

The suspension of the 3.0 RS also corresponded to that

developed for the 2.8 RSR, except that it retained the 2.7 RS's shorter struts. The tires were eight inches up front and nine in the back. Most intriguing was the retention of the 2.8 RSR's drilled and vented brakes.

The body of the 3.0 RS perpetuated the 2.8 RSR modifications, including its wider rear wheel arches, although there were a few telltale differences. The front dam retained the rectangular opening in the middle, but received two round openings on either side, both funnelling cooling air to the brakes. In the rear, where the 2.8 RSR retained the original duck tail, the 3.0 RS sported a wider, horizontal version, referred to as a "whale tail". Its increased size, which was made possible thanks to wide rubber edges, improved the lift factor to 11 pounds, down from 28.5.

One negative aspect of the 3.0 RS's increased width, as compared to that of the 2.7 RS, was that performance was only marginally improved. Zero to 60 mph took 5.2 seconds, while top speed was just over 150 mph. On the plus side, cornering capability increased dramatically.

Records show that 111 3.0 RSs were built. Of these, 42 were RSRs, while 15 conformed to IROC specifications. For Top

It was the last of Porsche's normally aspirated cars—the Turbo was already being readied...

Ten selection purposes, this left 59 RSs from which to make a final choice.

In an effort to narrow the options, the factory records received further scrutiny, and it was found that just six right-hand-drive cars had been built. Five went to England, while one went to Hong Kong.

In tracking down the cars delivered to Porsche's British dealer, one of them could not be located. Among the remaining four, number 99 stood out. It was found not only to be in pristine condition—having logged less than 14,000 miles—but to have belonged to James Hunt of Formula One fame.

The original owner was Lord Hesketh, in whose Formula One team Hunt sharpened his teeth as a driver. When Hesketh ran out of money, Hunt signed on with the Marlboro people, with whom he went on to capture the World Championship in 1974. The 3.0 RS is said to have been part of the final settlement between Hesketh and Hunt.

During this period, while he drove McLarens on the track, Hunt's mode of road transportation was the Porsche 3.0 RS. To make the car more comfortable during his high-speed continental trips, he exchanged the racing Recaro seats for more supportive

versions from the same manufacturer.

Later, number 99 was sold to Anthony Bamford, the well-known British connoisseur and collector of fine automotive machinery, who had the car repainted in silver. Before selling it a few years later, Bamford returned it to the original Canary yellow. The buyer was Paul Alexander, a worthy caretaker of such a preeminent machine, and a man whose skill behind the wheel is well documented in historic racing. In spite of the value of the car, Alexander still drives it hard, in that admirable British fashion.

The 3.0 RS, as a model, stands out as one of the rarest among road Porsches. It was, after all, duplicated only 59 times. Furthermore, it was the last true dual-purpose machine (not only perfectly legal for the road, but also homologated for Group 3 racing). And it was the end of Porsche's normally aspirated supercars—the Turbo was already being readied.

As an individual car, number 99 is the unchallenged Top Ten choice, virginal in its unabused state, and endowed with the magic touch of star quality. It is the best among the few that signalled the end of an era.

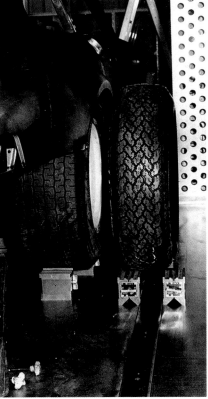

The 3.0 RS's engine lid hides a power plant that had been brought up to a 2993 cc displacement through a bore increase. Power rose from 210 hp to 230. The brakes were compatible to the performance, and came from the 917 racer. Their discs were drilled and ventilated, as can be seen in the photograph at the bottom of opposite page. Above, a photograph from 1972, when 11-inch rims were first tried out. The standard tire provides comparison. Note fender flare.

1976 930 TURBO

Inaugurator of the Turbo Generation

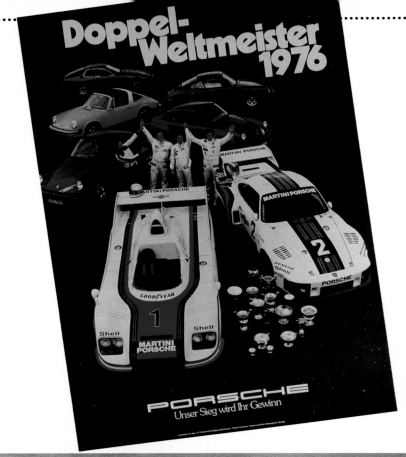

In the summer of 1975, at Porsche's Zuffenhausen facility, four cars were removed from the small series of U.S. 930 Turbos assembled prior to production. After shipping preparation, they were loaded onto a cargo vessel destined for the United States.

The serial number sequence of the U.S. specification 1976 Turbos was set to begin at 9306800001. According to factory records, the four cars shipped to the U.S. were numbers 011, 012, 013 and 014. Numbers 011 and 012 were engaged in display and photographic assignments, while 013 and 014 were used for U.S. type approval. After completion of their respective missions, they were sold as used cars.

These were the first U.S. specification examples of Porsche's new Turbo breed to reach American shores. As such, they were instrumental in pioneering a new era of prosperity for Porsche.

Just as Ferry Porsche—together with son Butzi and nephew Ferdinand—provided the driving force behind the creation of the basic 911, so did Ernst Fuhrmann, Porsche's chief executive since 1971, supply the spark and inspiration that led to the birth of the 930 Turbo.

Porsche had learned the lessons of turbocharging on the playground that had already witnessed so many of its major development triumphs—the race track. During the hunt for horsepower, the Weissach engineers had whipped their 917 Can-Am engines into putting out as much as 1100 hp— a near doubling of the power produced by the normally aspirated 917s.

In this formidable accomplishment, Fuhrmann recognized a key to the future— on the track as well as on the road. For the realization of these bold plans, he turned to his trusted fellow engineer in charge of research and development, Helmuth Bott, who in turn left the hands-on aspects of the turbo project to Norbert Singer and his staff.

Before the project could begin in earnest, however, it had to be determined whether the lessons learned in the United States could be applied to the European situation. The conversion formula provided by FIA for the handicapping of a turbo-charged engine allowed a volume no larger than 2142 cc. The question was: Could such a small engine compete? There was only one way to find out.

Nineteen seventy-six was a great year for Porsche's racing effort. Not only was the World Sportscar Championship brought home to Stuttgart by the 936, but the 935 managed to capture the World Championship for Manufacturers, making it a double affair. A Porsche poster, opposite page, commemorated the accomplishment. It was the first time a turbocharged machine had won the manufacturer's title, a fact that worked to increase interest in the new U.S. Turbo Carrera, an example of which is circling the Weissach test track in the photo on the opposite page. On this page, left, a birdseye view of the earliest known Turbo to reach the U.S. The survivor carries chassis number 014, and is our choice for the Top Ten spot. It is equipped with the largest and most elaborate among the whale tails, as can be seen in the photograph above. The primary grille allows cooling of the engine, while the secondary one, located on the tail, supplies air to the intercooler.

An animal, yes, but not an untamed brute like the RS; rather a domesticated breed with all the amenities...

Porsche's Turbo engine was a marvel of compact efficiency, as can be seen in the black and white photograph below, shot at the 1974 Paris Auto Show, where the new Porsche creation was introduced to the public. The color photos offer two further views of our Top Ten choice, while the Porsche poster reproduced to the right is proof that even in the land of Ferraris and Lamborghinis, automotive enthusiasts are not immune to Porsche prowess.

In the spring of 1974, when a down-sized turbo-charged engine was mated to an RSR chassis and body, the test results seemed promising. Proof of the pudding, however, lay in racing performance. Therefore, the equipage, piloted by Gijs van Lennep and Herbert Mueller, was sent to Le Mans, where it scored a sensational second. The incredible power of this special RSR becomes evident even from a quick glance at the performance figures: 500 hp at 8000 rpm, zero to 60 mph in 3.2 seconds, and a top speed—clocked at Le Mans' Mulsanne straight—of 189 mph.

After this success, the track appeared wide open for the completion of several more laps in the 911 development race. The first lap necessitated the creation of a high-performance street machine that could be homologated for Group 4 racing. The regulations now dictated that 400 units be built within a twenty-four month period. The result was the 930 Turbo, from which was derived the 934, 935, and 936 racers—a most successful constellation of Porsche racing stars.

For the road car, however, Fuhrmann envisioned a completely different animal than the one he had conceived for

the track—an animal, yes, but not an untamed brute, like the dual purpose RS; rather a domesticated breed with all the amenities a sophisticated driver could wish for.

As already stated, the birth of the 930 Turbo was the result of Fuhrmann's personal dedication. Just how much persistence it took to stay on course became apparent during the 1973 oil crisis.

Announced in October, the embargo resulted in a fit of financial turbulence that sent the world economy into a tailspin. Auto manufacturers cancelled projects, laid off workers and watched their inventory pile up in the storage yards. Long lines formed at gas stations and tough speed limits were hastily invoked everywhere. In Germany, authorities banned Sunday driving and limited Autobahn speed to 60 mph. The emergency decrees were so all-encompassing that they even included such facilities as Porsche's Weissach test track, hampering development of the street turbo.

These were indeed dark days for Porsche. From a production of 14,678 units in 1972-73, and a work force of 4,077, output for the 1974-75 period plummeted to 8,618,

Fuhrmann held the course, secure in his knowledge of what the market wanted, and confident that the tables would turn eventually...

Rear spoiler and wide fender flares, which all perpetuated the lines of that pioneer of aerodynamic efficiency-- the 3.0 RS--gave the Turbo Carrera a look of awesome potency. Yet, the evergreen shape of the 911 was not compromised. A few non-original items mar the appearance of our Top Ten choice. Among these are the wheels and tires. These irregularities, however, are on new owner Mark Palmer's short list of things to do.

and the number of employees to 3,386. For 1973-74, the profit-and-loss statement showed a break-even. Had it not been for the income from sales of spare parts, augmented by earnings from outside engineering assignments, a loss would have resulted.

Fuhrmann held the course, secure in his knowledge of what the market place wanted, and confident that the tables would turn eventually.

The styling of the 930 Turbo took its cue from the 3.0 RS, with its deep front air dam, its flaring front wheel arches, its bellowing rear dittos, and its wide, rubber edged whale tail. Standard-gauge steel was used for all body panels; there was no weight saving effort along the lines of the RS's.

Inside, the Turbo was luxuriously outfitted, with plaid or genuine leather as the upholstery materials of choice. Deep cut-pile carpeting covered the floor. A special touch was the "turbo" logo embedded into the carpet on the back of the left rear seat. Air-conditioning was standard.

The 930 rolled on fifteen-inch forged aluminum wheels. The rims were seven inches up front and eight in the rear. Tires were at first Dunlops, but were

later changed to Pirelli's new low profile P-7s, a product Porsche had helped develop. Although cross-drilled brakes had been used on the 3.0 RS, they were not initially fitted to the Turbo; quantity production techniques had not yet been perfected.

Suspension-wise, the 930 received a number of changes, mainly as a result of fine-tuning the geometry to compensate for wider wheels and greater power. New aluminum cross-members were deployed up front, and both torsion-bars and roll-bars were stiffened all around. Stiffer Bilstein shocks added the final touch.

In the engine compartment, turbo-charging changed the picture dramatically. The turbo itself, a KKK (Kuehnle, Kopp & Kusch) unit, was located on the left side, behind the engine, and close to the exhaust, from which it derived its propulsion. The complete engine unit was a marvel of efficient packaging, which was certainly a practical necessity as the new power plant had to fit into the space left by the vacated unit.

The engineers chose to work with the 3.0-liter version, leaving its 95 mm by 70.4 bore and stroke unchanged. For turbo duty, compression was set at 6.5 to one. Boost at 4500 rpm was

Palmer became intrigued by the low chassis number of his newly acquired Porsche Turbo...

If a formula could be devised to measure in numbers the relationship between luxurious accommodation and performance, Porsche's 930 Turbo would undoubtedly have topped the list of mid-seventies' contenders. Below, the camera peeks through the open window to reveal a 180 mph speedo and an 8000 rpm tach. At the bottom of the page, a full view of the working environment found in a Turbo tested by Road&Track.

11.5 psi, while peak power, 260 hp, was reached at 5500 rpm. Because of pollution control devices, the U.S. specification engine produced no more than 234 hp. It was so bloated by this equipment that the normally simple operation of removing plugs became painfully complex.

Nevertheless, the turbo package accomplished the trick, propelling Porsche's new flagship from zero to 60 mph in less than six seconds and to a top speed of 150 mph plus—numbers that reflected a rate of velocity that blew the doors off most other supercars.

For our Top Ten spot, we wanted an early example. A number of avenues were explored in our search for such a car, but not until we made contact with Pete Smith, former partner of Bob Smith Porsche in Hollywood, California, did we make progress. Smith recalled that, in the fall of 1975, he had obtained directly from the US Porsche distributor, one of the first Turbos imported to the country. The car had just over 4,000 miles on the odometer, a figure corresponding to the mileage required by California authorities in connection with state certification tests.

In a special arrangement with Porsche, Smith drove the machine for a period of time, submitting his impressions to the factory. He subsequently sold the car to Steve Earle, the man who gave us big-time racing nostalgia in the form of the Monterey Historic races. Earle used the car as his personal transportation for years.

Smith also put us in touch with the man who he thought owned the car today. Contacted, this man in turn told us he had given it a down-to-the-bare-metal paint job—fortunately not altering the original shade of *Oak Green*—and that he had soon afterward sold it to Mark J. Palmer of Berverly Hills, who still owns it.

Palmer, an architect—and a connoisseur of all things fast and beautiful—became intrigued by the low chassis number of his newly acquired Porsche. He contacted the factory for further information. The response established his car as one of the four shipped to the US in 1975—number 014.

Palmer has done extensive research trying to find the other three, but has so far not been successful. Number 014 remains the earliest known U.S. spec 930 Turbo in the United States, and therefore qualifies as a first rate survivor—as well as our Top Ten choice.

A peek in the Turbo's inner sanctum, the engine compartment, reveals a space filled to the bursting point. It seems no less of an accomplishment on the part of the creators to have engineered the system as such, but also to have made it fit in a space that had been devised for machinery of much less complexity. The color shot depicts the engine of chassis 014, while the black and white shot gives the factory view.

1986 959

Perfect Conveyor of Triple Purpose Concept

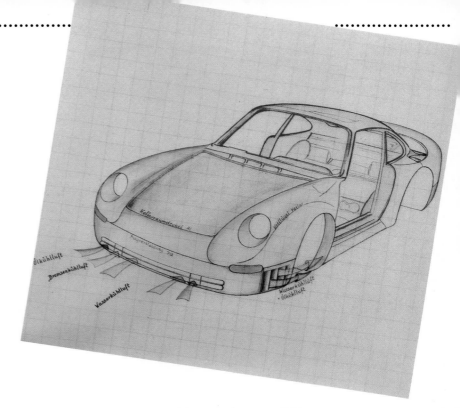

The road flows smoothly, faithfully tracking the contours of the narrow valley. Walls of dark pine forest, broken by clusters of beech and ash—their branches still bare—rush by on both sides. Looming tall, obscuring the morning sun, the trees cast cold shadows.

Our 911 Turbo, a factory press car, hums happily, moving at a steady clip. No need to slow down in the turns. Wide rubber and firm suspension keep the car steady as a rock.

We pass through a small village. The houses, built in an age-old German architectural style, seem to have originated from the identical mold, with wooden beams creating a geometric pattern of straight lines and diagonals within the rough plaster walls.

After the village, more trees, more shadows. Then suddenly the valley widens, opening to an expanse of pastures paved with brown winter grass. Bright patches of snow irritate our eyes. A stream, fast and furious from hillside run-off, snakes through the scenery. On a slope, bathed in warm spring sun, a sprinkling of buildings break the spell of serenity.

One of them, a large two-story structure, enhanced by a glassed veranda and terraced gardens, immediately catches our attention with its long conspicuous row of garage doors. We have arrived at our destination, the summer home of Professor Helmuth Bott, Porsche's famous former head of research and development, retired since 1988.

Warned of our visit, Bott comes to greet us with a warm, disarming smile. It becomes instantly clear that this super-star of the automotive universe does not assume the air of self importance often seen among executives at this level.

A young lieutenant in the Wehrmacht during World War II, Helmuth Bott spent the last turbulent months of the conflict in Hungary. For the next few years, while a down-and-out Germany struggled to get back on its feet, Bott supported himself as a school teacher.

Although Bott enjoyed teaching, his fascination with all things automotive soon took over. He applied for, and was accepted to, the auto mechanic apprenticeship program at Daimler-Benz.

After two years, with his basic education finished, Bott exchanged the Mercedes workshops for classrooms at the University of Stuttgart, where he enrolled in the mechanical engineering course. During this

The concept of the 959 was first put on paper in the rough form seen at the top of the opposite page. Bottom of the page, the full-scale styling study has taken shape, and, on this page, left, the 959 prototype--or Gruppe B— stands ready for shipment to Frankfurt, where it was introduced to the public. Below, our Top Ten selection: one of seven pre-production 959s, belonging to Helmuth Bott, the driving force behind its creation.

The shape of the 959 should not be judged on the basis of ordinary criteria. Had the stylists been given a free hand, the result would certainly have been different...

three-year period, as part of the program, he completed stints at Daimler-Benz's engineering office and the experimental department at Bosch.

In 1952, Bott was invited to join Porsche on a permanent basis as an assistant to the production manager. It was an association that would last thirty-six years, even longer when you count the period Bott spent as a consultant to Porsche after his retirement.

In 1954, Bott moved to the research and development department, where four years later he was placed in charge of chassis development. The duties included making his services available to the racing department. In this capacity, Bott traveled to most of the major races on the sports car calendar, including Targa Florio, Le Mans, and Daytona.

In 1968, Bott was entrusted with the execution of Porsche's ambitious expansion program at Weissach. Three years later, he took over management of the state-of-the-art facility, an assignment which included supervision of all the functions of research and development, including the work commissioned by other auto makers. Bott kept this position—and a seat on the board of directors beginning in 1976—until his retirement.

*I*n the early days of the sports car, going racing usually required nothing more than the removal of muffler, headlights, and bumpers. In time, however, the gap between performance levels of road and racing machines became so great it could no longer be spanned. By the early sixties, the dual purpose machine was a dying breed. Some of the last were produced by Porsche in the early seventies.

It is all the more remarkable, then, that Porsche a decade later undertook the creation of a dual-purpose machine. In fact, triple-purpose might better describe the bold ambitions of the Weissach wizards.

First, the 959 should be a modern road car, luxurious and civilized, with impeccable manners. Yet, it should be ready to race at a twist of the key. Second, it should, with proper equipment, be able to compete in Group B rally events, such as the Paris to Dakar. Also, by taking advantage of changes allowed by homologation rules, it should be possible to prepare the machine as a sports racer for events like Le Mans and Daytona. Third, the 959 should be a veritable showcase of the advanced technology Porsche envisions for future models— all while maintaining its

The 959 stands out not only as an exercise in engineering excellence, but as an example of exceptional styling. This aspect must be seen as all the more remarkable since its limits were set very narrowly, the object being to fuse aerodynamic requirements with the sacred 911 shape. Chief stylist Tony Lapine presided over a dedicated and gifted team: Wolfgang Moebius (exterior), Peter Reisinger (model creation), Arnold Ostle (interior), and Richard Soederberg (concept).

The sound comes rumbling like in a race car, but deeply muffled, emitting a fine metallic note that says sophistication rather than brute power...

On this spread, the 959 theme is represented in three different disguises and degrees of development. To the right, the 959 as a rally machine. The shot captures the Metge/Lemoyne team in the 1985 Paris to Dakar Rally, where all three Porsche entries came to grief. Having learned the lesson, Metge managed to drive his mount to victory the following year, with Ickx taking second. Below, the 959 in road disguise--potent, beautiful, unique.

911 ancestry. It was a tall order Professor Bott wrote for himself and his staff.

For power, the engineers built a flat six resembling the unit fitted in Porsche's 956/962 race car, including its four-valve layout, separate cam boxes, and titanium connecting rods. Unlike the racing engine, the 959 features two cylinder heads with three units in each, rather than six individual ones. Also, rather than duplicating the all-liquid cooling used on the 956/962, the 959 employs a mixture, with the cylinders being air-cooled in the normal 911 fashion, while the heads are water-cooled.

Desiring an instantaneous smooth surge of power, the engineers opted for twin turbochargers, of KKK manufacture, and fitted with individual intercoolers. The first unit cuts in at 1200 rpm, while the second joins the symphony at 4000. Running in unison, they race the scale in a whistling burst that builds to a crescendo at 8200 rpm and 28 psi.

With a bore and stroke of 95 mm by 67 creating 2850 cc, and compression of 8.3 to one, the 959 puts out 450 hp at 6500 rpm. An ample quantity of torque, in excess of 300 lb ft, is available already at 2200 rpm,

giving the 959 docility under normal traffic conditions. All this torque is transmitted to the road via a racing-type clutch and a six-speed gear box.

While the 959's spec sheet so far reads like the script for an automotive version of Alice in Wonderland, it is in the further description of the power train that its most innovative aspects are revealed.

From the gearbox, power is sent to the rear differential through a short shaft. A long shaft sends power forward to an electronically controlled clutch that allows infinite variation of tension. From here, power is transmitted further forward to a front differential. Four modes (traction, dry, wet, ice/snow), with a set of individual codes communicated to the special clutch and the rear differential via controls in the cockpit, produce a computer determined ratio of the amount of power conveyed to each axle.

The four-wheel drive, a concept explored by Porsche on the legendary Cisitalia Grand Prix machine already in 1948, combined with this new, revolutionary traction control system, elevates road holding, handling, as well as safety characteristics to previously unknown heights.

The black and white photographs show the versatile 959 in sports racing disguise--now with a 961 designation. To the right, the 1986 Le Mans 24-Hour race marked its debut. It was the first time a four-wheel drive car had qualified for the event, and, naturally, when the 961 captured seventh spot, winning its class, it was the first time such a car finished. Left, the 961 at the 1987 Daytona 3-Hours, where it did not fare so well. Faced with tire problems, it finished in 24th place.

Desiring an instantaneous, but smooth surge of power, the Porsche engineers chose twin turbo-chargers...

Porsche's most powerful road car engine is the focus of the photographs on this spread. Pictured below, the 959 power plant in splendid isolation. Opening the primary engine cover, which encompasses the entire width of the body and even incorporates the rear spoiler, reveals a tight fit and a host of auxiliary components. Opening two secondary lids, as illustrated in the scene at the bottom of the page, reveals the twin turbo units.

The brakes, of a four-piston, light-alloy type, internally ventilated and ram-air cooled, come from the 962 racer. An anti-lock system, built by Porsche and Wabco Westinghouse, completes the safety net.

Not to lag behind, the suspension also received its measure of innovative attention, which resulted in the scrapping of the familiar MacPherson struts up front and the torsion bars front and rear. The new setup features racing-type upper and lower wish-bones and dual Bilstein shocks in all four corners, with one unit in each pair electronically controlled.

The most novel suspension feature, however, is the variable ride height system. Three settings—normal measuring 120 mm, medium 150, and the maximum 180—provide levels to suit a variety of conditions. Developed primarily for rallying, the system is retained on the comfort version of the road car, but not on the sport version. At speeds over 100 mph, the system automatically returns ride height to normal level.

The shape of the 959 cannot be judged on the basis of ordinary criteria. After all, if the stylists had been given a free hand, the result would have been different. In this case, the parameters were narrow. It was a matter of integrating aerodynamic and engineering considerations into a pleasing package without disturbing the familiar 911 form.

The stylists needed the front to be low and narrow. Slicing off the tips of the fenders and slanting the headlights took care of the lowering. As far as the narrowing, the stylist's hands were tied; wide wheels, eight inches in front and nine in the back, needed flared fenders.

The windshield, the roof and the greenhouse follows the shape of the 911, with its galvanized steel monocoque chassis structure—properly modified to accept the altered transmission and suspension components—forming a skeleton for the outer skin. Aramid and fiberglass reinforced epoxy resin is used for all body components, except the doors and luggage compartment lid, for which an aluminum alloy is used, and the nose section, made from integral polyurethane foam. The composite material was also chosen for the full-length undertray, which is a key component in the search for ultimate aerodynamic efficiency.

A fully integrated and elegantly curved wing, growing out of the back fenders, puts the finishing touch to the rear as

So effective are the aerodynamic measures that a drag factor of 0.31 is achieved. More importantly, the lift is cut to zero...

well as to the entire creation, providing the 959 with its most prominent visual trademark.

The body sports a host of vents and ducts. Up front, a full-width grille admits cooling air to oil and water radiators. Oval nostrils, located just behind the door handles, funnel streams of relief to the intercoolers. Exits for the hot air are provided by slotted vents in each of the four corners of the body.

So effective are the aerodynamic measures that a drag factor of 0.31 is achieved. More importantly, lift is cut to zero.

The 959 was launched on January 21, 1983, when Helmuth Bott assigned the project to his deputy, Manfred Bantle. A prototype stood ready on October 9, a few hours before its Frankfurt debut.

Briefs explained Porsche's plans to build 200 copies for public consumption, plus a number of units for rally and circuit racing. Even with an indicated price tag of around 350,000 German Marks, it did not take long before the entire run had been reserved with deposits of 50,000 each.

It took Porsche much longer to bring the 959 to production, however. By the time deliveries could begin, in the spring of 1987, the price had risen to 420,000 Marks, translating to just under $200,000.

In 1986, the 959 fulfilled its promise as a superlative rally machine with an outright win in the Paris to Dakar event.

As a track racing machine, the 959 derivative—given a 961 designation—also lived up to its aspirations, although, without competitive classification, its full potential was never explored. Experiencing cooling problems during practice for the 1986 Le Mans, it finished the race in seventh place. Significantly, this was the first time a four-wheel drive design had competed in—and completed—the event.

Expectations were high for the Daytona 3-Hour race later in the season, but tire troubles robbed it of a place in the front row. The 961 returned to Le Mans in 1987, but failed to finish due to driver error.

When the 959 assembly line produced its last unit in the spring of 1988, the number of cars built totalled 234. Included among these were twelve test vehicles, seven pre-production units, and ten pilot cars, adding up to a total of 29 special units. It was in this limited category that we intended to concentrate our search for Top Ten candidates.

The step from drawing board to finished product went via a number of fifth-scale models, with which the basic shape, as well as various spoiler designs, were tested out in repeated wind tunnel sessions. On opposite page, a pre-production car is undergoing final testing in the Weissach tunnel. An important factor in reducing resistance and increasing side wind stability, was the cutting down of the fenders, which necessitated covered lights.

The speedometer, with its 340 kph termination point, gives the first-time driver a dose of the jitters...

Since it was the expressed goal of the 959 to take the 911 concept into the future, and since the 911 provided the basic chassis and body, it was natural that the interior also followed the familiar 911 tradition. Professor Bott's car, which was one of the first units built, received upholstery fabric left over from the early batches of 928s, seen to the right. Below, a Christmas tree of indication lights come on at a twist of the ignition key.

When our research revealed that Helmuth Bott owned one of these special units, the choice was as good as made. A fax was dispatched to Stuttgart to obtain his permission and cooperation for a photographic session, to which Bott agreed.

Bott's personal 959, the only example fitted with catalytic converter, carries number V6KOM, the V standing for *Vorserienwagen* or pre-production car, and the KOM for *Komfortversion*, which needs no translation. The car was used as a service training unit as well as a personal test car of Professor Bott's, whose guest drivers included Jackie Stewart, Mario Andretti, Jacky Ickx, Hans Stuck, and Walter Rohrl. The host was known to diligently grill these world class drivers for their impressions.

For the photographic session, we crossed the valley and went into the high country on the other side, where there were narrow roads between crew cut fields with very little traffic.

As we arrive back at the house, it starts to rain. We ask Professor Bott if he wants to cover the car, but he shakes his head, indicating that getting it wet is no big deal, which is lucky, because the silver surfaces are already dotted with rain

drops. We become aware of how persuasively the voluptuous body suggests power and speed. Suddenly its motionless state seems more imagined than real. We feel an urge to capture that notion on film. With rain pouring down, but protected under an umbrella, the camera zeroes in on the curvaceous silver shapes.

The rain will not let up. We ask Professor Bott if he wants to skip the brief test drive he had indicated would form the finale. Once again he shakes his head, engaging in a very animated description of how fool-proof the car is, and how it can be driven safely by anyone under any and all conditions.

Inside the cockpit, seats, dash and decor—all of the 911 configuration—feel reassuringly familiar, although the speedometer, with its 340 kph termination point, gives the first-time driver of this two-hundred-miles-per-hour-plus machine a dose of the jitters.

Out on the road, which skirts the valley in a series of curves and straightaways, the sound comes rumbling like from a race car, but deeply muffled, emitting just a fine metallic note that expresses sophistication rather than brute power. The controls feel smooth and easy, with the steering quicker than expected.

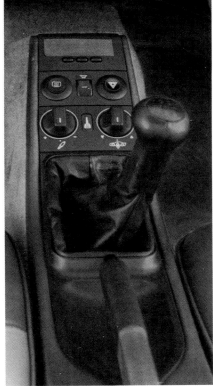

The plethora of technology and the electronic wizardry that characterizes the 959, does not clutter the dash with myriad dials and gauges, although there are some rather unusual ones. The photograph above, focuses on the dials seen immediately ahead of the shift lever. The one on the left controls the suspension setting, while the one on the right governs the ride height. On the opposite page, the gauge located to the far right of the panel deals with the drive program, which is engaged via a lever on the steering column.

Professor Bott sets the traction system for wet, then thrusts his fist forward in an unexpected explosion of force, indicating that it is time to punch the pedal...

The throttle response is crisp and immediate.

The rain comes down hard, washing the asphalt slick. The wipers sweep to the rhythm of a nervous beat. Professor Bott sets the traction system for wet, then thrusts his fist forward in an unexpected explosion of force, indicating that it is time to punch the pedal.

The machine takes off like a rocket, without any wheel spin. Full attention is necessary as everything seems to happen at once, the tachometer needle flipping, the need to shift to second, the tingling sensation in arms and legs, the second turbo cutting in, the need to shift to third, the comment from Bott that the car can do 90 mph in this gear, the need to let up on the throttle for the upcoming curve, the sudden apprehension as we enter the turn and the feeling of security as the machine seems to roll on rail where you would expect it to aquaplane.

A straightaway allows shifting into fourth. The torque comes through strong, with acceleration almost as vigorous as in second. A village comes up quickly, like an imagined scene in a distant Mille Miglia, but with trees instead of spectators lining the road.

We turn and drive back the same way we came, with Bott all the time urging faster cornering, as if he wants to prove that even the most inexperienced driver can do no wrong.

We are back at the house. The engine has been turned off. For a moment, there is only the splattering of rain and the ticking of cooling machinery. Then we hear our own voices, matter-of-factly discussing drive torque distribution and wheel slip recognition. Soon we realize that dusk is falling. Time is up. As we leave, there are thank yous and good-bys, all blended with that disarming smile.

We return the same way we came in the morning, heading northeast, towards Stuttgart. Our Turbo hums happily, rolling at a steady clip. The walls of dark forest sweep past on both sides of the road. Zooming through the village we notice that the window shutters have been closed against the elements. Streaks of yellow light show between the slats.

It has been a fine day. Although, regrettably perhaps, a cherished reality has been turned into a shattered fantasy, an illusion: The magnificent Turbo, one of the most potent machines money can buy, now feels like a timid proposition compared to the 959.

It took Porsche all of three years to bring the 959 to production. It must be remembered, however, that the task was a most monumental one, and that the result will stand the test of time. On the *opposite page*, a birds-eye view of part of the Roesslebau assembly area. To the left, Helmuth Bott, father of the 959, in discussion with Ferry Porsche and youngest son, Wolfgang. Below, Bott in retirement, flanked by a model of his crowning achievement.

1989 930 TURBO

The Last Slantnose is Shrine to the Breed

One historic day in May 1990, the Porsche factory made an unique drop-off at the Stuttgart air freight terminal. The shipment consisted of a one-of-a-kind automobile, so costly that an armed guard—brandishing a machine gun—was posted in the holding area while workers guided the special vehicle into a shipping container.

Accompanied by the armed guard, the container and its priceless cargo were trucked to the Frankfurt airport, where the unit was loaded onto a jet destined for San Francisco.

The extra rigorous security precautions did not end with the shipment's arrival in California. The armed guard remained with the car throughout unloading in San Francisco and subsequent forwarding by truck to Porsche's U.S. headquarters in Reno, Nevada, where final customs clearing took place.

Once the formalities were out of the way, the car set off on the last leg of its roundabout journey. This was by far the most time consuming stretch, as it went back across the North American continent by covered transporter to its destination, New York City. Here, the customer of the remarkable automobile, a Manhattan financier, awaited its arrival with great anticipation.

The object of all this fuss—a black 930S Turbo Cabriolet, chassis 070595—was not only the last Turbo off the line, but also the last Slantnose. As such, it was the subject of extraordinary consideration throughout the various steps of the building process; special treatment reflected in the extreme attention to detail, as well as in the fitting of an array of special equipment, all done at the factory—all accounting for a bottom line said to be in the area of half a million dollars.

Before delving deeper into the intricacies of this special Slantnose Turbo, we should take a brief detour to review Turbo production history as it unfolded subsequent to the model's introduction in 1975.

That first year saw a total of just 284 units come off the line, all for European consumption. In 1976, production rose to 1174, with 530 of these going to the U.S. The 3.3 liter came on line in 1978, and sales soared during the next three years, culminating in a 1979 record of 2552 units, only to drop drastically to 840 in 1980, the first year the Turbo was missing from U.S. showrooms. By the end of the Turbo decade, exactly 11,220 units had been built. The model made a U.S. return

Our Top Ten feature car, seen below, is not only the last 930 Turbo, but also the last Slantnose. A commemorative plaque, placed by Porsche inside the luggage space and pictured at the top of the opposite page, testifies to the fact. The Slantnose took its cue from a car specially built for Mansour Ojjeh. This car, seen to the left, was in turn inspired by the 935 racer, opposite page, although it featured the smaller version of this model's rear spoiler.

The Slantnose, or Flachbau in German, took its cue from a car the Porsche factory custom built for an oil-rich Arab...

in 1986, with the last few years adding 10,616 units.

Although the Turbo, in its 930 configuration, is history, its ferocious spirit lives on in the new 911 Turbo, a worthy successor that will add further prestige to the breed.

The Slantnose, or Flachbau in German, took its cue from a car Porsche built for an oil-rich Arab. This creation in turn was modeled after the 934 and 935 racers. It featured a slanting nose with retractable headlights. Front fender vents, located above the headlights, provided a cooling stream for the front brakes, while rear fender vents, placed just ahead of the wheels, funnelled air to the engine and rear brakes.

This outrageous machine created so much attention that specialist shops, such as Gemballa, Koenig, Strosek and many others began marketing independent conversions, which in turn prompted Porsche to offer its own conversion service, starting in 1981.

The orders were at first handled through the Customer Department at Works 1, where limited resources could manage only about 35 units per year. In 1986, the Slantnose conversions were moved to the Roesslebau plant, where they emerged

alongside the 959s at a rate of approximately 250 units a year. In this connection, the Slantnose became an official catalog item. Total production is thought to have been slightly more than one thousand units, of which only 237 were Cabriolets. The majority of the Slantnose cars went to the U.S.

When the Manhattan financier, to whose order the last Turbo was built, initially approached Porsche, it was simply to buy a normal Carrera for everyday use. His request for a genuine leather dash instead of the fake that was standard on U.S. models, however, put him on a collision course with, first, his local dealer, who informed him it was against company policy, then, Porsche Cars North America, who verified the fact.

Irked by this intransigence, the man from Manhattan directed letters to top officials at Porsche, among them Professor Ferry Porsche himself. Shortly afterwards, he received a call from Porsche clearing the way for a car personalized in any fashion he specified.

By this time, it had become clear that the Turbo was nearing the end. The Manhattan man thus changed his order to a Turbo, and was soon informed his would be the last built. As

On what was the longest outing since its epic journey by air from Frankfurt to San Francisco and by truck from San Francisco to New York, our Top Ten feature car was trucked to a high tech parking structure in Jersey City, a site where its muscular body could be decoratively juxtaposed with the facade of Manhattan's southern tip. Less than half a mile was added to the odometer during the photo session, and only ten minutes to the engine's running time, which is kept track of by a special gauge on the dash. The list of special touches and options on this machine, takes up no less than thirteen typewritten pages. No effort was spared by the Porsche factory to make this car, the last Turbo and the last Slantnose, an extraordinary creation.

Every knob, every switch, every bezel, every panel, is covered in leather, including the rear view mirror frame...

the Slantnose was also headed for extinction, the order was upgraded to include this special conversion. With these premises in place, the stage was set for the extraordinary effort on the part of the factory to make this machine exceptional.

Beginning at the heart of the matter, the engine received numerous power perks, among them Mahle pistons, high-performance heads, special crankshaft and flywheel, and Bosch Motronic dual fuel injection. In addition, it was balanced and polished for ultimate efficiency. It was dynamometer tested and far exceeded standard figures, although the specific numbers are not officially available.

The drivetrain was upgraded to include a similar six-speed transmission as used in the 959. The 17-inch wheels were specially ordered from BBS (custom made to accept wider tires without changes to suspension and wheel wells). A four-pipe exhaust system provided the finishing touch.

But it is really in the interior that the special effort is most obvious. As if wanting to put the leather dispute to rest for good, the upholsterers used the genuine article everywhere imaginable. Every knob, every switch, every bezel, every panel, is covered in leather, including the rear view mirror frame, hand brake lever, steering column, top lining and boot cover.

Three switches on the special center console operate electric doors that conceal an AM/FM tuner, a compact disc player, a digital audio tape player, and a preamplifier/equalizer. Crews from several of the world's leading audio component manufacturers spent weeks at the Porsche factory installing the state-of-the-art system.

Electronic features, such as a rain sensor that automatically raises the top and windows—even activates the alarm—the moment the mirror polished surfaces are struck by a drop of rain, is only one of the numerous special effects. A specially manufactured 220 mph speedometer, and an engine hour gauge (showing sixteen hours), do not seem out of place in this magnificent machine—one that was a natural Top Ten choice.

Instead of an everyday car, the man from Manhattan ended up with a collectible of the highest rank—a gem few will ever see in real life, however, as its owner has shown it publicly only once.

The convertible top mechanism of this special Turbo Slantnose is coupled to a sensor, which, when rain drops hit the body surfaces, will trigger its activation. The wheels are special BBS fare, chosen because they were not only the best money could buy, but also allowed the fitting of extra-wide wheels and tires without altering the suspension. This is no aftermarket special; all additional equipment was installed by the factory.

1989

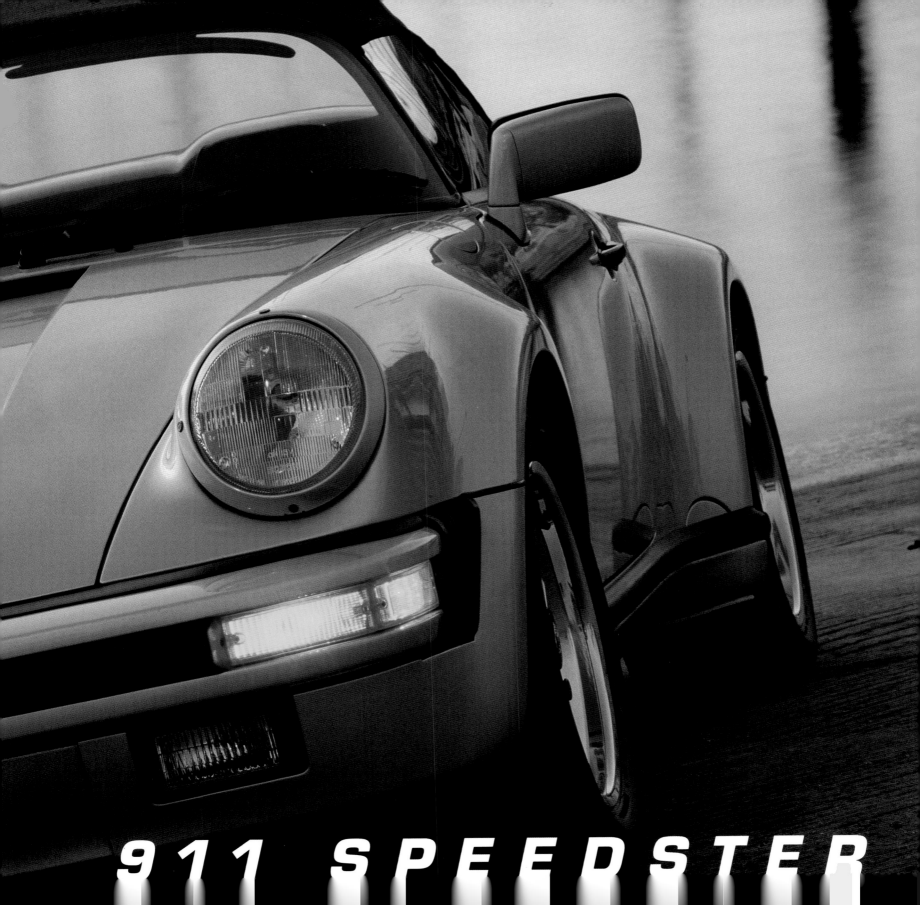

911 SPEEDSTER

Purveyor of the Past,
Prodigy of the Present

Visitors to the 1987 Frankfurt show, held in September, were intrigued by a sleek new Porsche convertible, featuring a low windshield and a curious double-bullet cover over the rear portion of the cockpit.

The model was not entirely new, however, not in the sense that it represented revolutionary technology. It was a cosmetic thing, a thing of nostalgia, a throwback to September 1954—the month and year when enthusiasts attending a concours at Watkins Glen, New York, first laid eyes on a new, stripped-to-the-bare-essentials Porsche.

This was the lovable little Speedster, a creature whose affordability and charm endeared it to a generation of sports car fans. It was a sure path to cult status. Thirty-three years later, Porsche chose to go down the same road, to the point of giving its new model the same name.

The spark that ignited development of the first-generation Speedster came from a German living in America, New Yorker Maximilian Hoffman, grand master among purveyors of exotic machinery. Besides inspiring the Speedster, Hoffman is credited with stimulating the creation of further legends, such as the

Mercedes 300 SL and the BMW 507.

In 1953, Porsche felt the pinch of competition from other sports cars making inroads on the U.S. market. Hoffman theorized that a more sporty and less expensive model could restore competitiveness. He was right in this assumption; between 1954 and 1958, almost five thousand Speedsters were sold, producing much-needed revenue for Porsche.

The second-generation Speedster was also, to a certain degree, inspired by a German American, Peter Schutz. With his parents, Schutz emigrated to Cuba in 1939—the year Hitler's tanks rolled into Poland, igniting World War II—before moving to Chicago in 1941.

Schutz earned a degree in mechanical engineering at Illinois Institute of Technology, Detroit. Stints with Caterpillar generated experience in engine development, which led to a career at Cummins. Here Schutz moved up through the ranks to become head of the truck engine division, and finally vice-president of sales and service for the U.S. and Canada.

In the late seventies, Schutz returned to Germany, where he subsequently advanced to the

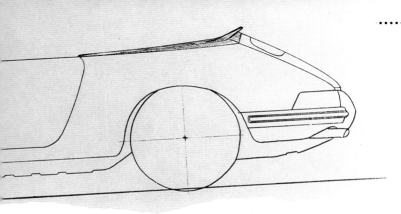

The rendering to the left, drawn in the early eighties, proves that the idea of producing a Speedster version of the 911, one to capitalize on the success of the 356 Speedster of the mid-fifties, was not a new one at Porsche. Note the virtually identical windshield shape of our Top Ten choice, below. This car was selected on the basis of having been featured in a photo layout on the French Riviera. Here it is at it again, this time in Santa Cruz, California.

But the Speedster concept refused to die. In 1986, Peter Schutz revived it in his own way, showing once again that anything was "do-able..."

board of Kloekner-Humboldt-Deutz, the Cologne-based industrial plant and machinery organization.

By the early eighties, Professor Porsche had become discouraged with Ernst Fuhrmann's leadership. As chief executive since 1971, Fuhrmann had promoted the development of front engine Porsches. Although he had given the 911 a shot in the arm with the Turbo, he no longer had a heart for the time-honored rear-engine concept. Fuhrmann moved inexorably towards elimination of the 911, a direction the founding father opposed.

It finally became clear that Fuhrmann had to go. Professor Porsche found a new chief executive in Peter Schutz who, with engineering background and sales experience from Porsche's most important market, seemed well suited. In addition, Schutz was both a sports car enthusiast and a believer in the sanctity of the 911. The change took effect on January 1, 1981.

Under Fuhrmann, the company line on the subject of a convertible 911 had been that the chassis could not handle the stress. This was nonsense to Schutz, whose motto "anything is do-able" soon became law.

Before long, several topless experimentals could be seen circling the Weissach test track. One of them was developed into a prototype and at the Geneva Show in March 1981, the public was treated to a first taste of the Schutz cuisine. The production Cabriolet arrived two years later.

Recent revelations show that the Speedster concept was kicked around at the same time as the normal convertible. From these discussions, the idea— driven by Helmuth Bott, chief of the research and development center at Weissach—evolved beyond the drawing board. Late in 1982, Tony Lapine, director of styling, finished a full-scale model based on a 911 SC; a prototype stood ready in the spring of 1983.

But that was as far as the idea went. It may not have been advisable from a marketing viewpoint to introduce two topless cars simultaneously. In any event, the prototype was hidden away in a Weissach garage.

But the Speedster refused to die. In 1986, Peter Schutz revived it in his own way, showing again that anything was "do-able". With the help of the Customer Department at Works 1, a 911 U.S.

Peter Schutz, an American of German descent, took office as the top man at Porsche in 1981, and soon activated the dormant Speedster. On opposite page, bottom, his idea of a Speedster, a one-off built by Porsche in 1986. Schutz drove it to and from work for several months, putting more than 4,000 miles on it. Opposite page, top, one of a series of renderings that formalized the production Speedster. The cover was already in place. As always, the end product did not look as good as through the artist's eyes.

Good looks are what the Speedster is all about, and that it accomplishes best with the top up...

specification Cabriolet was transformed into a Speedster-inspired convertible. The conversion is said to have taken 650 man hours. Schutz was so pleased with the result that he used the car for everyday transportation.

The final steps on the road to realization of the new Speedster were taken in June 1986, when Bott issued a development order, and in October, when management approved the concept for production. The first Speedsters rolled off the line in the fall of 1988.

The new Speedster differed from its classic counterpart in that it was not an economy model. It retained virtually all the amenities of the Carrera Cabriolet it was based on except, in order to cut weight, rear seats and electric window mechanisms were deleted. The difference in philosophy is illustrated by the original Speedster's cost of $2,995, which made it the lowest-priced Porsche at the time, compared to the new Speedster's sticker of $64,480, $5,280 more than that of the Cabriolet's.

Further weight reduction was achieved through the elimination of front quarter-windows and deployment of an unlined, hand operated folding

top. A total of 154 pounds of fat was shed. The 3.2 cc Carrera engine, which produced 214 hp at 5900 rpm, remained unchanged. But thanks to the loss of weight, the Speedster nevertheless added some performance sparkle to its sporty appearance, managing zero to sixty in about six seconds—half the time of the original—and a top speed of just under 150 mph.

The most important component of the Speedster redesign, however, was the new windshield. Manufactured from aluminum, it was about one inch lower than the standard version, and also leaned back five degrees further, which was crucial to recreating the classic speedster look.

Good looks were really what the new Speedster was all about. This it accomplished best with the top up, when it reproduced beautifully the menacing, hunkered-down stance of the original Speedster. The top-down aspect, on the other hand, revealed the double-bullet cover, an element adding a hump to the rear portion of the car, making it look tail heavy. Made of fiberglass, it was nevertheless a clever solution to a sticky problem. The cover, hinged at the rear, lifted up to allow stowage of the top,

The double-hump fiberglass cover was a clever solution to a tough problem, but did not improve the looks--the rear appeared too heavy. With the top up, on the other hand, the nostalgic spirit of the old Speedster was beautifully recalled, as evidenced by the color shots on this spread. The rendering at the top, shows another attractive solution, a hardtop--unfortunately never put into production. Also never built was a racing top, left, here demonstrated by Porsche racing ace Jochen Maas.

The adventure added 421 miles to the odometer—a figure still on the clock—as well as a touch of star quality...

Although the fiberglass cover and the low-cut windshield sets the Speedster apart visually from the Cabriolet, in the engine compartment, opposite page, matters are of common configuration. The windshield is one inch lower than that of the standard model, and raked back five degrees more, both measures contributing to the stimulating view from the driver's seat, below. Bottom of the page, the Speedster at speed, and right, its tonneau cover.

then snapped back in place, hiding the top and its folding mechanism.

When Speedster production closed in the fall of 1989, 2,104 units had been built. Of these, 165 were of the non-turbo look, lacking wide rear fender flares. Some 800 Speedsters were exported to the U.S.

The latter-day Speedster was a well-executed attempt on Porsche's part to add excitement to the last of its old-generation 911 line. Eager customers snapped them up, anxious to capitalize on the excellent investment potential.

When it came to choosing contenders for our Top Ten spot, we were immediately faced by this "investment factor". We found, for instance, that the uniqueness of a zero-mile car, was not unique at all. We needed something other than that to set a Top Ten choice apart—not an easy task, since with a new car, time has not yet separated the flowers from the weed.

Our research turned up a number of contenders, from which we chose a car first delivered to Holbert Porsche in Pennsylvania: number 173757. The car was subsequently transferred to the West Coast and a new owner.

Besides being just as pristine and perfect as the majority of 911 Speedsters we ran across, our Top Ten choice was selected by the factory for a trip to the French Riviera, where it was employed in an advertising photo session.

The adventure added 421 miles to the odometer—a figure still on the clock—as well as a touch of star quality.

While so many of Porsche's road car legends grew out of a need to satisfy racing homologation requirements— homologation specials—the 911 Speedster stemmed from a need to stimulate sales—a marketing special. As such, to the Porsche purist, the model carries a stigma of superficiality. But perhaps future generations will judge this as a perfectly acceptable criteria for greatness. The original Speedster indeed emerged from the same set of circumstances, although it certainly never attempted to build its reputation on imitating the past.

In any event, the 911 Speedster represents a limited edition issue, with all the ramifications which result from collectors' demand and ultimate value. As with wine, however, only time can tell how well it will age.

1990 911 CARRER

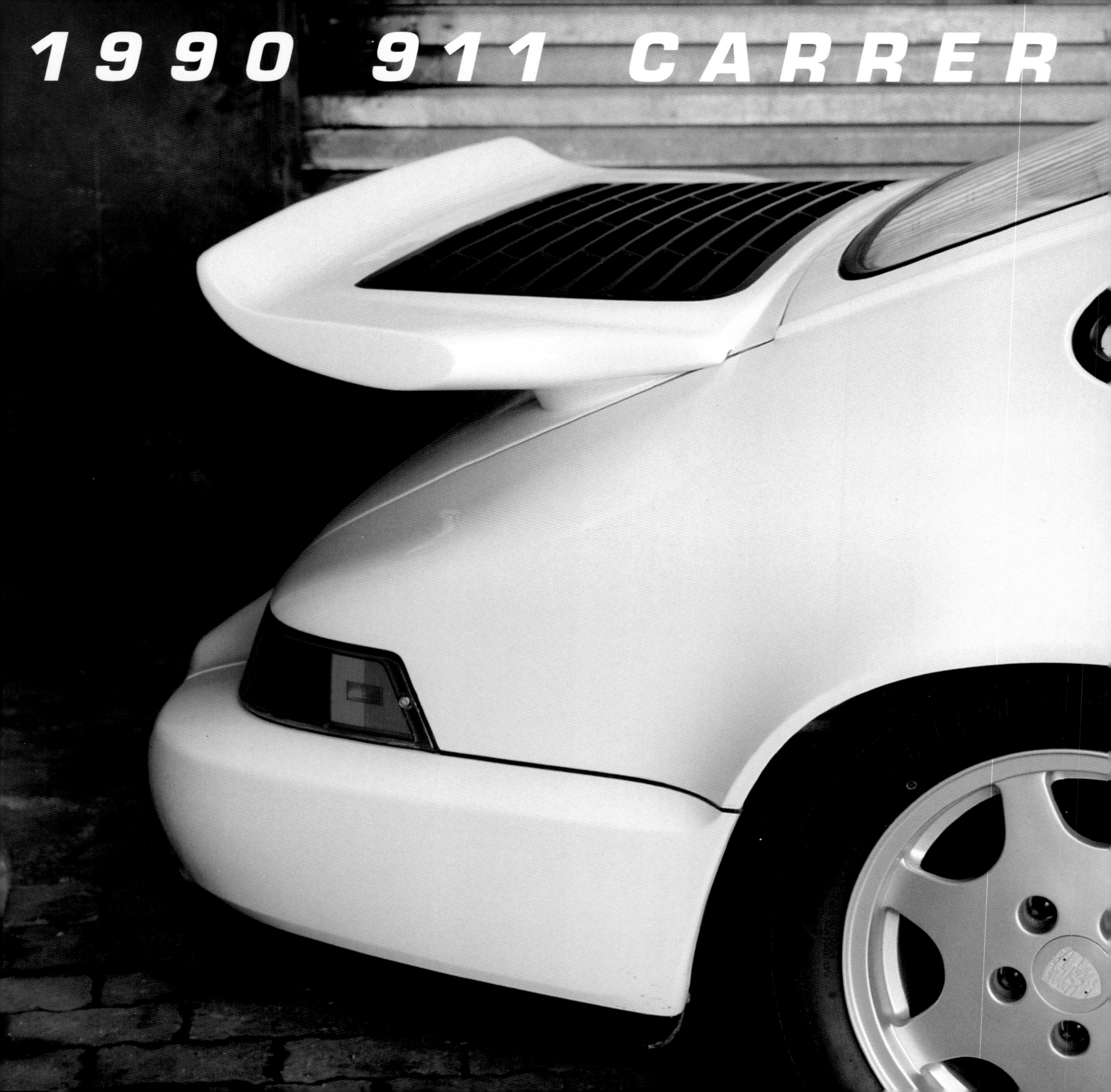

Limited-Edition Issue for the Fortunate Few

Villagers stand still on the tree-lined sidewalks, stopped dead in their tracks, stunned by the booming rapid-fire exhaust blasts from the white monster that rolls slowly down the main street of this small picturesque community, so quiet a moment ago.

Located somewhere between Ludwigsburg and Zuffenhausen, the village lies smack in the middle of Porsche territory. Perhaps some old-timer recalls the good old days when other loudmouths, Spyders and the like, might have roared by on peaceful country roads.

This day, however, what we are doing is both illegal and rude. Who knows, babies may be sleeping in upstairs rooms, behind open windows where lace curtains sway lazily in the afternoon breeze.

But there is no other way. For reasons artistic, we have to move the car from the garage that houses it, a location lacking photogenic qualities, to a truck terminal in the outskirts of the village that is infinitely more suitable as a backdrop for fast and powerful machinery.

Our partners in crime are Kerry Morse, a car enthusiast, collector, and automotive entrepreneur from Tustin, California who specializes in the purveyance of Porsche racing machines and parts, and Helmuth Greiner, from Ludwigsburg, a free-lance consultant to the Porsche racing department, veteran crew member of Porsche racing teams and caretaker of the object of our interest: a white 911 Carrera 4 Lightweight, or RS. An official designation has not been chosen or applied, since there is nothing official about this model in the first place.

Greiner is driving. Morse is back at the garage, trying to start his latest toy, a Trabant, the laughable little car that used to be the dream of East Germans but now is the latest fad of off-beat collecting. Last we saw Morse, he was pumping the gas pedal with great animation, grinning from ear to ear, surrounded by a blue cloud of exhaust fumes.

The Carrera 4 RS, as we will call it, is the brain child of Jurgen Barth, son of East German racer Edgar Barth, who escaped to make his free-world debut at the Nurburgring in 1957. Piloting a 550, he captured a fine fourth. Edgar's subsequent racing career was paralleled by his service as Porsche racing manager Huschke von Hanstein's right-hand man.

The evergreen Porsche 911 continues to display its competitive spirit in racing around the world, thrilling drivers and spectators alike. The poster, opposite, commemorates the British Porsche Club Championship series. The Carrera Cup was contested in Germany and featured equalized cars, seen to the left and at the bottom of previous page, the latter captured in action at the Norisring. Our Top Ten car, the first Carrera 4 RS, perpetuates classic 911 racing spirit.

The exhaust system features a separate stainless steel manifold for each bank of cylinders, tipped by a pair of minimal silencers...

The Carrera 4 RS uses as its basis the same chassis unit developed for the other 911 variations. Re-engineered for deployment in the new generation, it is produced using the most advanced techniques, right. The low-volume RS utilizes the same body panels as the Carrera 4, pictured in the two scenes below. The engine, depicted on the opposite page, is also shared with the Carrera 4, although the exclusive exhaust system adds fifteen horses.

The younger Barth has carved out an equally illustrious career for himself. A veteran of rallies like the Monte Carlo, as well as endurance events such as the Le Mans 24-Hours which he won in 1977, Barth is the man in charge of Porsche's Customer Sports Department at Weissach, where the Carrera 4 RS is built.

As soon as it became clear that four-wheel drive would be incorporated in the new 911 model line, Barth began toying with the idea of producing a lightweight version. It was a matter of tradition. The R, the RS, the RSR, all loomed large in his enthusiast mind.

When the Carrera 4 became available in the fall of 1988, Barth's daydreams became transformed into detailed plans. Armed with a presentation, Barth went to his boss, who subsequently gave the go-ahead to build a small limited series. Coincidentally, Morse was in Barth's office when the clear-signal came through over the phone. Intrigued, the American committed to the first handful of cars right there.

Greiner parks the RS between two cargo containers and turns off the engine. The sudden silence is almost as numbing as the shock of the ear-shattering start-up blasts. With the harshness of the salvos still ringing in our ears, we disembark to take a closer look at the machine.

In the back, below a fiberglass lid, lies the heart of the matter. The view inside the engine compartment does not differ from that of a normal Carrera 4. Greiner confirms that the RS indeed features the standard power plant, with its 3.6 liter capacity, 11.3 to one compression, dual ignition, electronic fuel-injection, and 6720 rpm power peak.

The single difference, one that can only be seen from underneath, is the exhaust system, which features a separate stainless steel manifold for each bank of cylinders, tipped by a pair of minimal silencers on each side. This alteration increases power from 250 hp to 265.

Closing the engine lid, we shift our focus to the exterior, and find that here, too, the differences from the normal Carrera 4 are few. Since wheel size (sixteen inches), and tire width (six inches up front and eight in the rear) remain unchanged, the body retains its basic shape. It does not need the wide turbo-style fenders, although the Turbo's whale tail

Squeezing into the tight Recaro racing seats, the driver is confronted by a minimal Momo steering wheel...

resides atop the engine lid where it constitutes the most obvious RS giveaway. Also, a look at the doors reveal that the roll-down windows have been replaced by fixed plastic panes with sliding inserts for ventilation.

One more detail indicates that this machine is not what it might appear to be at first glance. On the outside cowling, just ahead of the windshield, we find a red cut-off switch. As racing fans know, this is the visible part of a setup designed to deactivate the electrical system in the event of an emergency. It is obligatory for track work.

I t is in the Spartan interior, however, that we find the most obvious indications of the RS's special nature. Squeezing back into the Recaro racing buckets, each fitted with a five-point harness, we are confronted by a small Momo steering wheel. Beyond it, the instrument panel is dominated by a large rev counter. The clock has been removed. In its place is an instrument that warns of fan belt and alternator malfunction.

On the floor, in front of the passenger, we notice an oversized fire extinguisher. A sturdy rollbar arches above the

two seats (there are no rear seats). Everywhere we look, our scrutinizing eyes see painted metal surfaces; every ounce of sound-deadening material has been removed. Greiner tells us that 772 pounds were eliminated in the overall lightening effort, which includes the use of aluminum in doors and front lid.

I n the middle, mounted underneath the dash, two curious looking rotary knobs protrude. Greiner informs us that these are connected to special racing-type differentials, and can be used by the driver, while in motion, to adjust the distribution of power to front and rear, thus enabling him to achieve the desired balance between oversteer and understeer.

Also from the racing department come the clutch, a single-plate version with sintered metal lining, and the five-speed gear box (developed for the Paris-to-Dakar rally), with its shorter ratios for quicker acceleration.

A fter our brief introduction to the RS, we move on to the photography. A variety of angles, from atop a container, from flat on the ground, and from inside the cockpit of

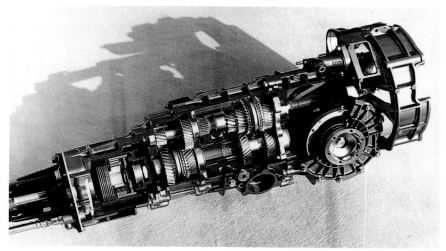

The whale tail and the Plexiglass side windows hint at the fact that this Carrera 4--the two color pictures on the spread showing it from a bird's eye view--is a very special machine. The RS sprang from the enthusiast mind of the man Porsche selected as head of its Customer Sports Department, Jurgen Barth, whose credentials are perfect. Above, he is seen with his father Edgar, while learning the ropes as a Porsche apprentice. Opposite page, a cut-away view of the Carrera 4 transmission.

Accelerating at full blast, exploding to sixty in a fiery burst lasting less than five seconds, peaking in a thunderous roar at one hundred thirty—these are the best ways to experience this machine...

The Porsche factory poster reproduced here, serves as an illustration of the extremes in the Carrera 4 model range, with the Cabriolet epitomizing fast motoring in elegance and comfort, and the RS representing high-speed travel in its most brutal form. To the right, the RS's interior is as stark as can be, with all comfort features completely removed. Below, the instruments stay unchanged; the seats are replaced by tight, racing harnessed Recaros.

a truck, are explored and executed. As we pack up, Morse arrives in his Trabant. He is not only still accompanied by a blue cloud but also by a timid sputtering from its 26 hp engine.

After another brief introduction—to the Trabant—we return to the Porsche. Morse reaches for the ignition key. A simple cardboard tag dangles from the key ring. He holds it up, pointing. It has a hand-written number on it: 01—the first Carrera 4 RS. It is the reason we are here. Certainly, no other example is better qualified for the Top Ten spot.

Number 01 belongs to Frank Gallogly, who lives in New Jersey. The car has to stay in Germany because the complete absence of emission gear renders the RS unwelcome in the U.S. Morse informs us that 02 is in Japan, 03 and 04 in Germany, and 05, also in Japan. The whereabouts of 06 is not known, but 07 belongs to an American who, like Gallogly, keeps it stored in Germany. Number 08 is in England, while 09, 10 and 11 are under construction at Weissach.

The RS is an ultra collectible, special (an unofficial model) and rare (less than one dozen produced). Yet, it is an anomaly, a model in search of a clear

purpose. It is exceptional both for what it is, and for what it is not. It is a race car. Yet, it is not. There is no obvious venue for which it was designed. It is a road car and with an exhaust system it can be registered in most countries. Yet, it cannot be imported to the U.S.

Regardless of its purpose, the RS, with its interpretation of the best of the new-generation 911, is a piece of art worth owning—if one can afford a price twice that of a Turbo.

On the way back to the garage, Morse drives the RS. It is clear from the look on his face that he hates having to tread so softly on the throttle. Accelerating at full blast through the gears, exploding to 60 mph in a fiery burst lasting less than five seconds, peaking in a thunderous roar at 130—these are the obvious ways to experience this machine.

Greiner follows in the Trabant. Pedestrians again stand stopped in their tracks, this time not only baffled by the noise but captivated by the contrast of the two cars—one reflecting a system where the urge to achieve went without reward, the other a society where a grown-man's toys can cost as much as a house with a swimming pool.

PORSCHE 911 *Carrera 4 Cabriolet*

1991 911 TURBO

Heir to the Tradition, Harbinger of the Future

Our photography and road test session started out with an episode that fused past and present in a most appropriate fashion.

We had just finished the formalities necessary to release a 1991 911 Turbo from the press pool into our temporary possession. With keys at the ready, we proceeded from the second floor of Works 1—where Porsche's public relations department is located—down to the ground level.

Works 1 happens to be the oldest facility in the Zuffenhausen complex, left over from the early days when Ferdinand Porsche directed his successful automotive consulting firm from these premises. Built in 1938, the building saw feverish activity during the war years. One of the creations stemming from the Zuffenhausen engineering center was the *Kubelwagen,* Germany's parallel to America's Jeep. Although dark and dreary in light of today's emancipated architectural style, the building still constitutes hallowed ground to a Porsche devotee.

These days, in addition to public relations and other support functions, Works 1 is home to the customer service department, where new cars are

prepared for customers choosing factory delivery, and where maintenance and restoration work is performed. Also in this building, on the second floor, is the office of Ferry Porsche—who in 1984 was awarded the same honorary title as his father, that of professor. Fittingly, it is the same suite once occupied by the senior Professor.

We finally manage to locate our red Turbo parked among other cars by a fence that runs along the four-lane public road dividing the factory grounds into an old and a new section. After stowing our camera equipment and looking over the gauges and controls— noting that they follow the familiar Porsche pattern—we find ourselves caught in one of two parallel queues of cars that move in a stop-and-go fashion toward the gate house and its boom. It is lunchtime.

A dark green 928 moves up on our right. Both side windows are rolled down all the way, as are the windows in our equipage. Behind the wheel sits a man whose distinctive features we immediately recognize. The jowls have become fuller with age, the wrinkles more deeply engraved, but the eyes still

More than five decades separate the photographs on this spread. To the left, Ferdinand Porsche, father of such divergent cars as the Volkswagen and the Auto Union racer, is engaged in a discussion with German pre-war racing ace Bernd Rosemeyer. Opposite, Ferdinand's son, Ferry, father of the automobile that carries the family name, braves the lens in a recent portrait. Below, the newest 911--catapulting the classic concept into the future.

It was left to Ferry to keep the bloodline pure; he did not hesitate to take drastic measures to steer the ship back on the right course...

The new Turbo retains its trademark whale tail, both for maintenance of the sporting image and for the stability needed at the higher speeds attained by the force-fed machine as opposed to the normally aspirated, right, which sports a smaller spoiler that extends or retracts automatically depending on the speed. Below, the engine and its turbocharger work smoother than ever. Cleaned up front and rear makes for the best looking 911 to date.

possess their trademark expression, that familiar look of deep concern, mirroring the thoughts of a man preoccupied with finding creative solutions to complicated problems.

The man is none other than Professor Porsche himself, still going strong in his eighty-second year. Today, like his co-workers, he is taking time out for lunch. As we stare, unable to conceal our surprise at suddenly being faced with the founding father, he turns toward us, and with a hardly noticeable smile utters a polite "malzeit". The word is not readily translatable into English, but is similar to the French "bon appetite".

Without Ferry, there would not have been a Porsche sports car. Ferdinand Porsche, Ferry's father, had expressed interest in starting his own car company in the twenties, but there was never enough money to fund such a venture in those financially tumultuous times.

Ferry toyed with the concept of a Porsche sports car during the years immediately preceding the war. It was his penchant for sporty driving that provided the impetus. During 1933 and 1934, he became a successful rally competitor with his two-liter Wanderer. When war broke out, he owned both an Alfa and a BMW. But as far as building a sports car of his own, the timing, for obvious reasons, was not right.

When the time came, it was left to Ferry alone to make the dream come true. Immediately after the war, his father, accused of war crimes, spent nearly two years incarcerated in France. The allegations were later dropped, but the experience weakened his health, and his involvement with the birth of the Porsche sports car was limited to that of an advisor. He died in 1951, a few months after his 75th birthday.

It was also left to Ferry to keep the blood line pure. A number of men served him ably at the helm of his firm. But when, as was the case with Ernst Fuhrmann, there was a deviation from the original direction, Ferry did not hesitate to take drastic steps to steer the ship back on course.

Today, with his youngest son Wolfgang—nicknamed Wolfi—at his side, Ferry is still in control. Seeing the founding father, not in some figurehead role, but in a trivial day-to-day situation, was indeed revealing. The latest incarnation of his sporting spirit, the 911 Turbo—

After nearly three decades in a rapidly changing and extremely competitive market place, there is still no question whatsoever as to the origin of the latest generation 911 styling; Butzi Porsche's original creation--developed by this gifted Ferry Porsche offspring in the early sixties--is still very much in evidence, as can be gleaned from the Porsche factory shots to the lower left and right. Wider wheels and the resulting increase in body width, does wonders for the evergreen machine.

Despite its familiar exterior, the latest 911 Turbo is a virtually new car. Just fifteen percent of the parts carry over from the old...

which we were just starting to experience—ties together the ends of a line that he unfurled forty-four years earlier.

Despite its familiar exterior, the 911 Turbo is a brand new car. Just fifteen percent of the parts carry over from the old 930 Turbo.

The new Turbo is based on the Carrera 2, and shares this latest 911 generation's chassis structure, its basic suspension, its interior, as well as its re-designed body panels.

But the Turbo's suspension received special attention. Semi trailing arms were reinforced, shocks stiffened, springs and struts tightened, and anti-roll bars thickened. In addition, wider wheels and rims were specified, which preserved the classic Turbo look, with its wide rear wheel arches. The brakes also received special attention. Already equipped with ABS in its Carrera 2 form, the drilled and ventilated discs of the Turbo were endowed with a swept area thirteen percent larger than before.

The new Turbo did not get a new engine, however. This will most likely be the next step. Thus, for now, the power plant is not the 3.6-liter unit used in the Carrera 2, but the faithful

3.3-liter unit that has been around for a decade and a half, although now thoroughly updated.

New intake manifold, bigger turbocharger, and revised exhaust system—externally manifested by twin exhaust pipes—increased the flow capacity. Without touching bore and stroke, the Weissach engineers thus managed to add thirty-three horses, for a new grand total of 315 hp. A larger intercooler and a lighter turbo impeller—the latter assuring quicker throttle response at low speeds—completes the overhaul.

As a result, the zero-to-sixty time stands improved by two seconds, to a stimulating 4.8, and the top speed by five mph, to an exhilarating 168 mph, making the new Turbo the fastest road 911 yet, not counting the 959, which we see as a homologation special and a test bed for advanced engineering, rather than a normal catalog issue.

But the new Turbo is not only the best performing, it is also the best looking, thanks to a thorough re-design. Gone are the unsightly bumpers, the windshield is smoothly bonded-in for better aerodynamics, and under the car, a flush floor

The 911 has indeed proven its mettle as a long distance runner when it comes to its basic shape. With some of its design elements created as early as 1959, that shape is now more than three decades old. Over the years, there have been numerous updates, in particular items such as bumpers, spoilers and flares. These have often looked a bit contrived, added on--which they truly were. With this latest generation 911, the body stylists have managed to integrate the elements into a most pleasing whole. Helping to cement this impression is the fact that, after all these years, the spoilers and the flares have indeed become a Porsche axiom. The philosophy of gradual updating has been applied to the interior as well.

Car enthusiasts can rest assured that the classic Porsche theme will be with us for a long time, well into the next century...

The wheels of the Turbo take their cue from a design developed for the 959. Their impressive size--17 inches--and muscular form, complement the styling of the new flagship. Curving spokes, separated by sizeable openings, propel ample amounts of cooling air to the brakes, which are dimensioned to give all the stopping power needed; four-piston calipers grip huge vented discs, 12.68 inches wide up front, 11.77 inches in the rear.

pan further increases the slipperiness, all producing a drag coefficient of 0.36. This aspect could have been better had it not been for the whale tail. The continued deployment of this Turbo trademark was a given, however, not only for the sake of image, but the huge fin acts as a rudder, improving stability at high velocity. Furthermore, without it, there would have been no room for the intercooler.

The search for a Top Ten car initially focused on the first Turbo built, a machine tested by Georg Kacher in the December issue of the British magazine *Car.* But the equipage proved elusive. It had vanished without a trace. The factory was of no help in the matter. Its policy of not giving out information about a specific car other than to its owner, gave us a fit as well as a case of Catch 22.

The car we finally chose, chassis number 470082— presumably the eighty-second built—turned out to be endowed with a distinction of its own, however, in that it was the same machine originally tested by Jerry Sloniger, the veteran Porsche scribe, and featured in his article appearing in the February 1991 issue of *Excellence* magazine.

Well out on the road, however, we forgot all about serial numbers and dead-end confrontations. The Turbo manifests its groomed and refreshed self in the form of a new and delightful attitude. No longer is there a risk of falling victim to heart failure when entering a corner with too much lead on the pedal. Instead of having a tendency to become derailed, as was the case with the old Turbo, the new Turbo stays firmly on the track.

Another idiosyncrasy of the old Turbo was the sudden kick in the rear from the turbo cutting in. Although an endearing novelty to some, it certainly did not make for smooth driving. The new Turbo still shows a bit of lag in getting off the mark, and the progression of the turbo can still be felt under brisk acceleration, but the power delivery is more controllable.

With the new Turbo, Porsche's Weissach wizards have not only created a worthy successor to the tradition, but have also shown that it was possible to take the 911 envelope further than anyone ever expected.

Porsche enthusiasts can rest assured that the classic Porsche theme will be with us for a long time, well into the next century.

Configuration:
Six-cylinder, air-cooled,
opposed (boxer).

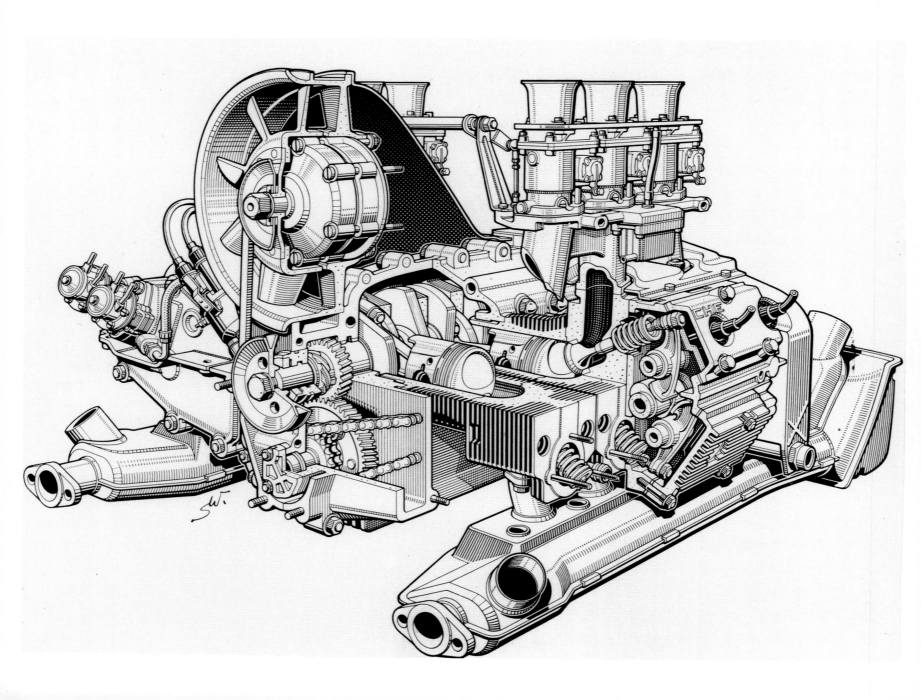

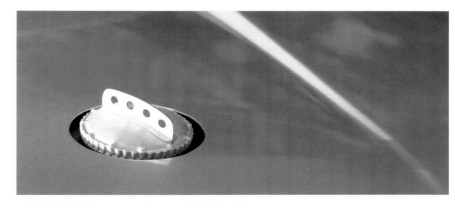

1964 Porsche 911

Engine

Designer: Ferdinand Pieche, Hans Tomala, Klaus von Rucker.
Configuration: Air-cooled, six-cylinder, horizontally opposed (boxer).
Bore and stroke: 80 mm by 66.
Displacement: 1991 cc.
Cylinder block: Light alloy.
Cylinder heads: Light alloy.
Valves: Two per cylinder.
Valve actuation: One overhead camshaft per bank, finger-type rocker arms.
Pistons: Light alloy.
Crankshaft: Forged steel, running in eight main bearings.
Lubrication: Dry sump.
Electrical system: Twelve volt, single-point breaker distributor.
Compression ratio: 9 to 1.
Carburetion: Two triple-choke Solex overflow carburetors.
Power: 130 hp at 6100 rpm.

Drive train

Transmission: Five-speed, manual, all-synchromesh, rear mounted inboard of engine.
Clutch: Single dry-plate.
Final drive: Fully articulated drive shafts, spiral bevel differential.

Chassis

Wheelbase: 87 inches.
Frame: Pressed steel platform in unit with body.

Front suspension: Independent, MacPherson struts and lower wishbones, longitudinal torsion bars, tube-type shock absorbers.
Rear suspension: Independent, semi-trailing arms, transverse torsion bars, tube-type shock absorbers.
Steering: Rack and pinion.
Brakes: Four-wheel discs.
Wheels: Steel, 15-inch, 4.5-inch rims front and rear.
Tires: 165/70 front and rear.

General

Styling: Butzi Porsche.
Drag coefficient: 0.38.
Body: Steel.
Assembly plant: Zuffenhausen.
Number produced: 232. (1964 model year).
Period built: September 1964 to December 1964.
Dimensions: Overall length 164.5 inches, width 63.5 inches, height 52 inches.
Weight: 2185 pounds.
Fuel tank capacity: 16.5 gallons.
Fuel consumption: 14/19 mpg.
Zero to 60 mph: 9 seconds.
Top speed: 132 mph.
Bottom line: $6,500.

1967 Porsche 911 R

Engine

Designer: High-performance modifications by Hans Mezger.
Configuration: Air-cooled, six-cylinder, opposed (boxer).
Bore and stroke: 80 mm by 66.
Displacement: 1991 cc.
Cylinder block: Light alloy.
Cylinder heads: Light alloy.
Valves: Two per cylinder.
Valve actuation: One overhead camshaft per bank, finger-type rocker arms.
Pistons: Light alloy, chromed cylinders.
Crankshaft: Forged steel, running in eight main bearings.
Electrical system: Twelve-volt, semi-transistorized Marelli ignition, two plugs per cylinder.
Compression ratio: 10.3 to 1.
Fuel feed: Two triple-choke IDA Weber carburetors.
Power: 210 hp at 8000 rpm.

Drive train

Transmission: Five-speed, manual, rear-mounted inboard of engine.
Clutch: Single dry-disc type.
Final drive: Spiral bevel, limited-slip differential.

Chassis

Wheelbase: 87 inches.
Frame: Pressed steel platform in unit with body.

Front suspension: Independent, single lower A-arms, tube-type shocks, longitudinal torsion bars, MacPherson telescopic struts, anti-roll bars.
Rear suspension: Independent, semi trailing links, transverse torsion bars, tube-type shock absorbers, anti-roll bar.
Steering: Rack and pinion.
Brakes: Four-wheel discs, vented.
Wheels: Fuchs alloy, 15-inch, 6-inch rims up front, 7-inch rear.
Tires: Front 165/70, rear 215/60.

General

Body: Steel, aluminum, and fiberglass.
Assembly plant: Porsche racing department.
Number produced: 20 (plus four prototypes).
Production period: Fall 1967.
Dimensions: Overall length 164.5 inches, width 63.5 inches, height 51 inches.
Weight: 1830 pounds.
Fuel tank capacity: 22 gallons.
Fuel consumption: Not available.
Zero to 60 mph: Not available.
Top speed: Not available.
Bottom line: Not available.

1973 Porsche 911 Carrera RS

Engine
Designer: High-performance development by Hans Mezger.
Configuration: Air-cooled, six-cylinder, opposed (boxer).
Bore and stroke: 90 mm by 70.4 mm.
Displacement: 2687 cc.
Cylinder block: Light alloy.
Cylinder heads: Light alloy.
Valves: Two per cylinder.
Valve actuation: One overhead camshaft per bank, finger-type rocker arms.
Pistons: Light alloy, Nikasil cylinders.
Crankshaft: Forged steel, running in eight main bearings.
Lubrication: Dry sump, thermostatic oil cooling.
Electrical system: Twelve-volt.
Compression ratio: 8.5 to 1.
Fuel feed: Bosch mechanical fuel-injection.
Power: 210 hp at 6300 rpm.

Drive train
Transmission: Five-speed, manual, rear-mounted inboard of engine.
Clutch: Single dry-plate.
Final drive: Spiral bevel, limited-slip differential.

Chassis
Wheelbase: 89.5 inches.
Frame: Pressed steel platform in unit with body.
Front suspension: Independent, MacPherson struts, single lower A-arms, longitudinal torsion bars, Bilstein gas/oil shocks, anti-roll bar.
Rear suspension: Independent, semi trailing links, transverse torsion bars, Bilstein gas/oil shocks, anti-roll bar.
Steering: Rack and pinion.
Brakes: Four-wheel discs, vented.
Wheels: Fuchs alloys, 15-inch, 6-inch rims front, 7-inch rear.
Tires: Front 185/70, rear 215/60.

General
Styling: Anatole Lapine and the Porsche design staff.
Drag coefficient: 0.40.
Body: Steel, fiberglass.
Assembly plant: Zuffenhausen.
Production period: July 1972 to July 1973.
Number produced: 1580 (204 Sport version).
Dimensions: Overall length 164 inches, width 63.5 inches, height 52 inches.
Weight: 2400 pounds.
Fuel tank capacity: 22.5 gallons.
Fuel consumption: 17/22 mpg.
Zero to 60 mph: 5.5 seconds.
Top speed: 153 mph.
Bottom line: $8,750.

1974 Porsche 911 Carrera RS

Engine
Configuration: Air-cooled, six-cylinder, horizontally opposed (boxer).
Bore and stroke: 95 mm by 70.4 mm.
Displacement: 2993 cc.
Cylinder block: Light alloy.
Cylinder heads: Light alloy.
Valves: Two per cylinder.
Valve actuation: One overhead camshaft per bank, finger-type rocker arms.
Pistons: Light alloy.
Crankshaft: Forged steel, running in eight main bearings.
Lubrication: Dry sump, oil-cooler in left front fender.
Electrical system: Twelve-volt.
Compression ratio: 9.8 to 1.
Fuel feed: Bosch mechanical fuel-injection.
Power: 230 hp at 6200 rpm.

Drive train
Transmission: Five-speed, manual, rear-mounted inboard of engine.
Clutch: Single dry-plate.
Final drive: Spiral bevel, limited-slip differential.

Chassis
Wheelbase: 89.5 inches.
Frame: Pressed steel platform in unit with body.
Front suspension: Independent, MacPherson struts, single lower A-arms, longitudinal torsion bars, Bilstein gas/oil shocks, anti-roll bar.
Rear suspension: Independent, semi trailing links, transverse torsion bars, Bilstein gas/oil shocks, anti-roll bar.
Steering: Rack and pinion.
Brakes: Four-wheel discs, cross-drilled, vented.
Wheels: Fuchs alloys, 15-inch, 8-inch rims up front, 9-inch rear.
Tires: Front 215/60, rear 235/60.

General
Styling: Anatole Lapine and the Porsche design staff.
Body: Steel, fiberglass.
Assembly plant: Zuffenhausen.
Number produced: 59.
Production period: July 1973 to March 1974.
Dimensions: Overall length 167 inches, width 70 inches, height 52 inches.
Weight: 2410 pounds.
Fuel tank capacity: 21.5 gallons.
Fuel consumption: 11/13 mpg.
Zero to 60 mph: 5.2 seconds.
Top speed: 152 mph.
Bottom line: Approximately $25,000.

1976 Porsche 930 Turbo

Engine
Designer: Turbo development under the direction of Hans Mezger and Valentin Schaeffer.
Configuration: Air-cooled, six-cylinder, opposed (boxer).
Bore and stroke: 95 mm by 70.4 mm.
Displacement: 2994 cc.
Cylinder block: Light alloy.
Cylinder heads: Light alloy.
Valves: Two per cylinder.
Valve actuation: One overhead camshaft per bank, finger-type rocker arms.
Pistons: Light alloy.
Crankshaft: Forged steel, running in eight main bearings.
Lubrication: Dry sump.
Electrical system: Twelve-volt, breakerless ignition.
Compression ratio: 6.5 to 1.
Fuel feed: Bosch K-Jetronic fuel-injection.
Power: 234 hp at 5500 rpm.

Drive train
Transmission: Four-speed, manual, rear-mounted inboard of engine.
Clutch: Single dry-plate.
Final drive: Spiral bevel, limited-slip differential.

Chassis
Wheelbase: 89.4 inches.
Frame: Pressed steel platform in unit with body.

Front suspension: Independent, MacPherson struts, single lower A-arms, longitudinal torsion bars, gas shocks, anti-roll bar.
Rear suspension: Independent, triangular trailing links, transverse torsion bars, gas shocks, anti-roll bar.
Steering: Rack and pinion.
Brakes: Four-wheel discs, vented.
Wheels: Forged alloys, 15-inch, 7-inch rims front, 8-inch rear.
Tires: Front 185/70, rear 215/60.

General
Styling: Anatole Lapine and the Porsche design staff.
Drag coefficient: 0.40.
Body: Steel.
Production plant: Zuffenhausen.
Number produced: 530 (1976 US specs).
Production period: September 1975 to August 1976.
Dimensions: Overall length 169 inches, width 70 inches, height 52 inches.
Weight: 2785 pounds.
Fuel tank capacity: 21 gallons.
Fuel consumption: 24 mpg.
Zero to 60 mph: 6.1 seconds.
Top speed: 156 mph.
Bottom line: $26,000.

1986 Porsche 959

Engine
Designer: Helmuth Bott and Manfred Bantle.
Configuration: Mixed air- and water-cooled, six-cylinder, horizontally opposed (boxer).
Bore and stroke: 95 mm by 67.
Displacement: 2850 cc.
Cylinder block: Light alloy.
Cylinder heads: Light alloy.
Valves: Four per cylinder.
Valve actuation: Two overhead camshafts per bank, finger-type rocker arms.
Pistons: Light alloy.
Crankshaft: Forged steel.
Lubrication: Dry sump, twin oil-coolers.
Electrical system: Twelve-volt, solid-state ignition.
Compression ratio: 8.3 to 1.
Fuel feed: Bosch Motronic fuel-injection system.
Power: 450 hp at 6500 rpm.

Drive train
Transmission: Six-speed, manual, rear-mounted inboard of engine.
Clutch: Single dry-plate.
Final drive: Computer-controlled variable-torque-split, four-wheel drive system.

Chassis
Wheelbase: 89.4 inches.
Frame: Pressed steel platform combined with steel cage.

Front suspension: Independent, upper and lower A-arms, coil springs, twin shock absorbers, anti-roll bar.
Rear suspension: As up front.
Steering: Rack and pinion, power assisted.
Brakes: Four-wheel discs, cross-drilled, vented, anti-lock.
Wheels: Magnesium, 17-inch, 8-inch rims front, 9-inch rear.
Tires: Front 235/40, rear 255/40.

General
Styling: Wolfgang Moebius and the Porsche design staff.
Drag coefficient: 0.31.
Number produced: 234.
Body: Kevlar, fiberglass, aluminum, and polyurethane.
Assembly plant: Zuffenhausen.
Dimensions: Overall length 167.5 inches, width 72.5 inches, height 50.5 inches.
Weight: 3190 pounds (Touring).
Fuel tank capacity: 22.5 gallons (Touring).
Fuel consumption: 11/13 mpg.
Zero to 60 mph: 3.9 seconds.
Top speed: 196 mph.
Bottom line: Approximately $250,000.

1989 Porsche Turbo 930 S

Engine
Configuration: Air-cooled, six-cylinder, opposed (boxer).
Bore and stroke: Not official.
Displacement: Not official.
Cylinder block: Light alloy.
Cylinder heads: Light alloy.
Valves: Two per cylinder.
Valve actuation: One overhead camshaft per bank, finger-type rocker arms.
Pistons: Light alloy.
Crankshaft: Forged steel, running in eight main bearings.
Lubrication: Dry sump, front-mounted large-capacity oil-cooler.
Electrical system: Twelve-volt, breakerless ignition.
Compression ratio: 7 to1.
Fuel feed: Dual Bosch Motronic fuel-injection.
Power: Not available.

Drive train
Transmission: Six-speed, manual, rear-mounted inboard of engine.
Clutch: Single dry-plate.
Final drive: Quaife torque sensing differential.

Chassis
Wheelbase: 89.4 inches.
Frame: Pressed steel platform in unit with body.

Front suspension: Independent, MacPherson struts, single lower A-arms, longitudinal torsion bars, Bilstein shocks, anti-roll bar.
Rear suspension: Independent, triangular trailing links, transverse torsion bars, Bilstein shocks, anti-roll bar.
Steering: Rack and pinion, power assisted.
Brakes: Four-wheel discs, cross-drilled, vented, power assisted.
Wheels: BBS specials, 17-inch, 7.5-inch rims front, 10-inch rear.
Tires: Front 215/40, rear 255/40.

General
Styling: Anatole Lapine and the Porsche design staff.
Body: Steel.
Production plant: Zuffenhausen.
Number produced: 237 Cabriolets.
Production period: 1986 to 1989.
Dimensions: Overall length 170 inches, width 70 inches, height 49 inches.
Weight: Not available.
Fuel tank capacity: 21 gallons.
Consumption: Not available.
Zero to 60 mph: Not available.
Top speed: Not available.
Bottom line: Not available.

1989 Porsche 911 Speedster

Engine
Configuration: Air-cooled, six-cylinder, horizontally opposed (boxer).
Bore and stroke: 95 mm by 74.4 mm.
Displacement: 3164 cc.
Cylinder block: Light alloy.
Cylinder heads: Light alloy.
Valves: Two per cylinder.
Valve actuation: One overhead camshaft per bank, finger-type rocker arms.
Pistons: Light alloy.
Crankshaft: Forged steel, running in eight main bearings.
Lubrication: Dry sump.
Electrical system: Twelve-volt, breakerless ignition.
Compression ratio: 9.5 to1.
Fuel feed: Bosch LE Jetronic fuel-injection system.
Power: 214 hp at 5900 rpm.

Drive train
Transmission: Five-speed, manual, rear-mounted inboard of engine.
Clutch: Single dry-plate.
Final drive: Limited-slip differential.

Chassis
Wheelbase: 89.4 inches.
Frame: Pressed steel platform in unit with body.

Front suspension: Independent, MacPherson struts, lower A-arms, longitudinal torsion bars, tube shocks, anti-roll bar.
Rear suspension: Independent, triangular trailing links, transverse torsion bars, tube shocks, anti-roll bar.
Steering: Rack and pinion, power assisted.
Brakes: Four-wheel discs, vented, power assisted.
Wheels: Alloys, 16-inch, 7-inch rims front, 9-inch rear.
Tires: Front 205/55, rear 245/45.

General
Styling: Anatole Lapine and the Porsche design staff.
Body: Steel.
Production plant: Zuffenhausen.
Number produced: 2104.
Production period: September 1988 to August 1989.
Dimensions: Overall length 169 inches, width 70 inches, height 49 inches.
Weight: 2600 pounds.
Fuel tank capacity: 22.5 gallons.
Fuel consumption: 18 mpg.
Zero to 60 mph: 6.0 seconds.
Top speed: 150 mph.
Bottom line: $65,480.

1990 Porsche Carrera 4 RS

Engine
Design: Under the direction of Paul Hensler.
Configuration: Air-cooled, six-cylinder, opposed (boxer).
Bore and stroke: 100 mm by 76.5 mm.
Displacement: 3605 cc.
Cylinder block: Light alloy.
Cylinder heads: Light alloy.
Valves: Two per cylinder.
Valve actuation: One overhead camshaft per bank, finger-type rocker arms.
Pistons: Light alloy.
Crankshaft: Forged steel, running in eight main bearings.
Lubrication: Dry sump.
Electrical system: Twelve-volt, breakerless ignition.
Compression ratio: 11.3 to1.
Fuel feed: Bosch Motronic port fuel-injection.
Power: 265 hp at 6100 rpm.

Drive train
Transmission: Five-speed, manual, rear-mounted inboard of engine.
Clutch: Single dry-plate type.
Final drive: Four-wheel, individually adjustable torque distribution.

Chassis
Wheelbase: 89.4 inches.
Frame: Pressed steel platform in unit with body.

Front suspension: Independent, MacPherson struts, lower A-arms, coil springs, tube shocks, anti-roll bar.
Rear suspension: Independent, triangular trailing links, coil springs, tube shocks, anti-roll bar.
Steering: Rack and pinion, power assisted.
Brakes: Four-wheel discs, vented, power assisted.
Wheels: Cast alloy, 16-inch, 6-inch rims up front, 8-inch rear.
Tires: Front 205/55, rear 225/50.

General
Styling: Harm Lagaay and the Porsche design staff.
Body: Steel.
Production plant: Weissach.
Number produced: 10 (still in production).
Production period: Beginning August 1989.
Dimensions: Overall length 168.5 inches, width 65 inches, height 52 inches.
Weight: 2425 pounds.
Fuel tank capacity: 20.5 gallons.
Fuel consumption: Not available.
Zero to 60 mph: Not available.
Top speed: Not available.
Bottom line: About $200,000.

1991 Porsche 911 Turbo

Engine
Design: Updating under the direction of Paul Hensler.
Configuration: Air-cooled, six-cylinder, opposed.
Bore, stroke: 97 mm by 74.4.
Displacement: 3299 cc.
Cylinder block: Light alloy.
Cylinder heads: Light alloy.
Valves: Two per cylinder.
Valve actuation: One overhead camshaft per bank, finger-type rocker arms.
Pistons: Light alloy.
Crankshaft: Forged steel, running in eight main bearings.
Lubrication: Dry sump, oil cooler on crankcase, additional front-mounted oil-cooler .
Electrical system: Twelve-volt, EZ ignition, two spark plugs per cylinder.
Compression ratio: 7 to1.
Fuel feed: Bosch K-Jetronic fuel-injection.
Power: 315 hp at 5750 rpm.

Drive train
Transmission: Five-speed, manual, rear-mounted inboard of engine.
Clutch: Single dry-plate type.
Final drive: ZF slip-limiter.

Chassis
Wheelbase: 89.4 inches.
Frame: Pressed steel platform in unit with body.

Front suspension: Independent, MacPherson struts, lower control arms, coil springs, anti-roll bar.
Rear suspension: Independent, semi-trailing arms, coil springs, anti-roll bar, automatic toe correction.
Steering: Rack and pinion, power assisted.
Brakes: Four-wheel discs, vented, cross-drilled, power assisted, ABS.
Wheels: Cast alloy, 17-inch, 7-inch rims up front, 9-inch rear.
Tires: Front 205/50, rear 255/40.

General
Styling: Harm Lagaay and the Porsche design staff.
Drag coefficient: 0.36.
Body: Steel.
Production plant: Zuffenhausen.
Number produced: 600 first-year production.
Production period: Beginning August 1990.
Dimensions: Overall length 168.5 inches, width 70 inches, height 51.5 inches.
Weight: 3275 pounds.
Fuel capacity: 20.5 gallons.
Fuel consumption: 21 mpg.
Zero to 60 mph: 4.8 seconds.
Top speed: 168 mph.
Bottom line: $95,000.

Porsche, Ferdinand Anton Ernst...

ACKNOWLEDGEMENTS

Last, But Not Least...

The author wishes to extend his appreciation to the following individuals and organizations in recognition of their important contribution to this book.

First on the list comes fellow author and Porsche historian Bruce Anderson, whose massive knowledge and vast network of contacts proved invaluable during the process that led to the establishment of the particular cars to be featured.

Further valuable assistance was provided by Fred Hampton, London, England; Kerry Morse, Tustin, California; and Thomas Wenner, Zurich, Switzerland, who generously shared of their time and enthusiasm.

The author especially enjoyed the opportunity to visit with one of the most notable names in the Porsche community, Helmuth Bott, Porsche's former head of research and development, who graciously took time out for a photo session, expertly narrated test drives, a delightful lunch, and an afternoon of illuminating conversation.

The historic photographs, posters, brochures, drawings, come from two primary sources: The Porsche photographic archives, where librarian Klaus Parr helped with the research, and Road & Track, where assistance was provided by librarian Otis Meyer.

The color photographs are by the author, who used Kodak Ectachrome Professional Plus 100 film, which was run through a Mamiya RZ 67 camera. Two lenses were mostly at work, a 110 mm normal, and a 250 mm telephoto. Laboratory services were provided by Newell Colour of San Francisco, and Custom Color, Glendale, California.

In addition to the car owners, named in the contents section, the author also wishes to thank the following for their special assistance: Frank Barrett, Ulrich Beger, Carmen Berrio, Bruce Canepa, David Colman, Bob Fleming, Norbert Grabotin, Helmuth Greiner, Tim Johnson, Rolf Koch, Larry Morris, John Paterek, Ray Paterek, Klaus Otto Reikert, Allen Seymour, Pete Smith, and Rolf Sprenger.

In addition to the portion of the author's work that depended on primary research, for his secondary sources, works of the following authors were found of great value: Bruce Anderson: Porsche 911 Performance Handbook; Dean Batchelor: Porsche Buyer's Guide; R. M. Clarke: The Brooklands Books on Porsche; Michael Cotton: Porsche Progress—Stuttgart's Modern Development Story; The Porsche 911 and Derivatives; Paul Frere: Porsche 911 Story; Chris Harvey: Porsche 911 In All Its Forms; Jurgen Lewandowski: 959; Brett Johnson: The 911 & 912 Porsche—A Restorer's Guide to Authenticity; Karl Ludvigsen: Porsche—Excellence Was Expected; Chris Poole and the Auto Editors of Consumer Guide: The Complete Book of Porsche; Ferry Porsche and John Bentley: We At Porsche; John Starkey: The Racing Porsches— R to RSR.

Color separation, printing and binding was provided by Book Builders, Hong Kong.

Finally—last but not least—the author wishes to thank Tom Toldrian and Jackie Kramer, of Top Ten Publishing Corporation, who were responsible for final editing of the manuscript.

THE

1   2   3   4   5

TOP

6   7   8   9   10

TEN